W9-AUY-495

North African Cooking

North African Cooking

EXOTIC DELIGHTS FROM MOROCCO, TUNISIA, ALGERIA, AND EGYPT

Hilaire Walden

CHARTWELL
BOOKS, INC.

A QUINTET BOOK

Published by Chartwell Books
A Division of Book Sales, Inc.
PO Box 7100
Edison, New Jersey 08818-7100

This edition produced for sale in the U.S.A., its
territories and dependencies only.

Copyright © 1995 Quintet Publishing Limited.
All rights reserved. No part of this publication may be
reproduced, stored in a retrieval system or
transmitted in any form or by any means, electronic,
mechanical, photocopying, recording or otherwise,
without the permission of the copyright holder.

ISBN 0-7858-0267-3

This book was designed and produced by
Quintet Publishing Limited
6 Blundell Street
London N7 9BH

Creative Director: Richard Dewing
Designer: Ian Hunt
Project Editor: Claire Tennant-Scull
Editor: Lesley Ellis
Photographer: David Armstrong

Typeset in Great Britain by
Central Southern Typesetters, Eastbourne
Manufactured by Eray Scan Pte Ltd, Singapore
Printed by Leefung Asco Printers Ltd, China

ACKNOWLEDGMENTS

Quintet Publishing would like to thank The Kasbah,
London, for providing North African ceramics and
metalware; also Evergreen and Gorgeous, London
N16, for providing flowers for photography

Location photography by Nick Bailey and Life File

Contents

Introduction

Bordering the southern Mediterranean Sea are the three countries of Algeria, Morocco and Tunisia, which were once known as the Maghreb and today make up the region of North Africa.

The cuisine of this region is now popular throughout the world – evocative, colorful and sophisticated, it is full of the romance of North Africa, and rich with the flavors of warm spices.

Together the three countries of North Africa offer a very distinctive style of cookery, with many similarities and shared themes that cross the region: slow-simmered, spicy casseroles called *tagines,* for example, are found throughout the area, as are steamed dishes of *couscous* grains, aromatic lamb recipes, colorful and astonishingly sweet desserts and sweetmeats, and pies and pastries made from a special wafer-thin pastry called *warka.*

Each country has its own unique characteristics, of course; its own favorite spices and national dishes: Moroccans like full, rich flavors, and often include saffron in their cooking; Tunisians have a penchant for more highly flavored, fiery dishes; while Algerians prefer their dishes rather less spicy.

North African cuisine has its roots in many different places and ancient cultures. The succession of different peoples who have invaded, traded with or visited North Africa over the centuries have all left their legacies: the Persians contributed a predilection for combining meat and fruit; the famous pigeon pie called *b'stilla* was brought from Andalusia via the Moors; and Tunisian *chakchouka,* a dish of pepper, tomato and egg, has its origins in Turkish *menemen.*

Two thousand years ago the countries of Morocco, Tunisia, Algeria and Libya were just one country, known as the Maghreb. It was the home of Christians, the pale-skinned, fair-haired and fine-featured nomadic Berbers. The diet and traditions of the Berbers and the nomadic Bedouin Arabs are still evident today in the use of dates, *smen* (a cooked and aged butter) and grains. Ingenuity stemmed from necessity and centuries ago the Bedouin people discovered the versatility of different grains. They discovered how to use fermented grains as a natural "starter" to produce leavened breads, and some sources claim that they developed dried pasta as a way of preserving dough during their long treks

RIGHT *Imposing North African landscape silhouetted by cloudless, intense blue skies*

RIGHT *Tinmel Mihrab, Morocco*

across the desert, and then took it with them when they landed in Sicily, from where it spread to the rest of Italy.

North Africa has a long coastline so there has always been easy access for traders and invaders. In the first century BC, Phoenician traders arrived and introduced dried sausages, forerunners of the spicy little Algerian sausages called *merguez,* which had been devised as a way of preserving meat during the traders' lengthy journeyings. Next came the Carthaginians who were responsible for introducing durum wheat and its byproduct, semolina. This was adapted by the Berbers into *couscous,* which is today a staple of the area.

With the invading Arabs of the seventh century came the Muslim religion which since then has become the strongest cultural influence in the region, dictating food as well as every other aspect of life. The Arabs, who had long been the spice merchants of the world, also brought many exotic spices such as saffron, nutmeg, ginger, cloves, and cinnamon from the Spice Islands.

Moors returning voluntarily, or expelled, from Spain brought back the foods of Andalusia such as olives and olive oil. Fruits such as oranges, plums, and peaches also crossed the Mediterranean.

In the 14th century it was the turn of Turkish Ottomans, who brought them sweet and delicate pastries. Later, European traders and colonizers arrived and relics of their influence include tea from British merchants, who disposed of large quantities in Tangiers and Mogador when they were seeking new markets during the Crimean War.

Today, restaurant menus may be written in Spanish, English, or French. French sophistication has been absorbed into the essence of the Maghreb. French is spoken in all three countries, particularly Algeria, which was occupied longest by the French. Middle-class Algerians speak French in preference to Arabic and housewives buy French-style baguettes rather than Arabic *kesra.*

Some ingredients, now so characteristic of North African cooking, were originally imported from the New World: tomatoes, potatoes, zucchini, and chilies and peppers which also yield the paprika and cayenne pepper so important to the local cooking.

Eating in North Africa

Hospitality is important to the people of North Africa and meals are prepared as abundant offerings to family, friends, and even casual passers-by who drop by or are invited to come in; and many varied dishes are set on the table. Ancient rituals of eating have been kept alive by nomadic tribes. Feasts at which *mechoui* (spit-roast whole lamb) is the main dish are still enjoyed by the Bedouins. *Mechoui* has been adapted in cities, and the lamb is halved or quartered before being roasted over a brazier.

In middle-class North African homes meals are served with formal elegance. Bright mosaics decorate the walls of the dining room and there are richly woven carpets, Baroque silverware and hand-carved furniture. Diners sit at low tables (*tbla* or *mida*) and, in silence, a servant or young member of the family will take a bowl of perfumed water around the diners in turn, holding it beneath their hands and pouring water over them from an *ied ettas;* a towel is then proffered.

Food is traditionally eaten with the thumb, forefinger and middle finger of the right hand (the left hand is considered unclean); to eat with one finger is considered a sign of hatred, to eat with two shows pride, three accords with the Prophet Mohammed, while to eat with four or five fingers is a sign of gluttony.

Bread is used to help mop up the cooking juices and sauces, and to carry the food to the mouth. Wheat in the form of couscous and bread, not rice, is the main staple of the diet.

In a land where literacy levels have been very low, cooking knowledge and recipes have been handed down by word of mouth from mother to daughter. Cooking has always been considered women's work and a North African wife spends much of her time preparing food. On occasions of family feasts, female relatives and friends all gather in the kitchen to help with the preparations, and so share and pass on their recipes, experience, and knowledge.

Cooking Equipment

North African kitchens are very simple with the minimum of equipment; labor is cheap and plentiful so tasks are done by hand, not with gadgets. Ovens are rare, even in restaurant kitchens. Food to be baked is taken to the neighborhood communal oven. There is also a lack of weighing equipment; measuring is done by eye and feel.

There are no chairs in a traditional kitchen, and often even a table is absent; cooks squat when both mixing and cooking on the brazier. There may be just a stool or two perhaps, or even an old carpet folded to act as a seat for the cook. In the average traditional country kitchen the most usual equipment to be found is:

COUSCOUSIER consists of two parts, a tin, aluminum, stainless steel, or earthenware bottom part (*gdra*) in which to cook meat, poultry, and vegetables, and a *kskas,* the top part. This holds the *couscous* and has a perforated base and sits snugly on the *gdra* so the steam from below permeates and flavors the grain. A saucepan with a tightly fitting colander, or a steamer can be used instead.

GENBURA a glazed earthenware pot, which is very broad in relation to its height; used for storing water.

GHORBAL a sieve with a perforated leather bottom for gauging the coarseness of semolina.

GSAA a large, flat wooden or unglazed earthenware dish with a 4 inch sloping lip which is used for mixing dough for cakes, breads, and pastries, and to mix and aerate semolina grains for *couscous.*

KHABIAS fairly high but not very wide earthenware jars, glazed on the inside, for preserving meat and storing flour, corn, and pulses.

MGHORFA a large wooden spoon.

M'IDOURNA OR T'BECK a round, flat basket which can also be used for aerating semolina grains for *couscous.*

ABOVE *Women selling earthenware pots in Oued-Laou market, Morocco*

ABOVE *Brassware at Marrakech market, Morocco*

MEHRAZ a heavy brass mortar and pestle for pounding spices and herbs (wood is not used as it would soon become tainted).

QA TAGINE a deep copper dish in which a *tagine slaoui* is placed when it is served, to protect the table.

TAGINE SLAOUI also often known simply as a *tagine,* this is a round earthenware pot with a glazed lid shaped like a coolie's hat, which is used to cook stews of meat, fish, poultry, or vegetables. In North Africa, *tagines* are cooked over charcoal but if using a traditional earthenware *tagine* over the direct heat of a gas or electric hob it is best to use a heat diffusing mat to protect it (but check with the handbook for electric cookers).

There will also probably be a few copper *taouas* (casseroles) in most kitchens, a pan for frying fish or almonds, knives and earthenware bottles for keeping spices.

For cooking on there is a small round charcoal brazier, usually round and of unglazed earthenware, called a *kanoun* or *mjmar,* specially designed to hold the round bottom of a *tagine* safely in place with its three raised points. The low, even heat that can be achieved with a charcoal fire is ideal for the slow-cooking *tagines* need if they are to be at their most succulent and flavorsome. This type of heat is also ideal for allowing richly flavored sauces to simmer very gently, but charcoal can also be adjusted to give a fiercer heat for cooking kebabs, brochettes, and fish.

Other traditional equipment includes a large basket with a decorated pointed lid called a *t'bicka,* which is used for serving bread; a *t'bsil dial warka,* which is a large round flat tin-covered dish with a shallow rim that is used, bottom-side up, for baking *warka* and bottom-side down, to bake *b'stilla.*

Flavors of North Africa

CHERMOULA a distinctive mixture of onion, cilantro, garlic, chilies, and spices widely used to bring character and flavor to many dishes. *Chermoula* is used as a marinade for broiled, baked or braised fish, poultry, lamb, and game such as rabbit. The combination and proportions of ingredients vary from cook to cook, and also according to the kind of food to be marinated and the character of dish required.

See page 126 for basic *Chermoula* recipes that can be used in other recipes.

COUSCOUS is made from semolina that has been ground, moistened and rolled in flour. Most *couscous* now on sale is pre-cooked and needs only to be moistened and steamed to heat through and separate the grains. Butter is usually rubbed into *couscous* to help separate and enrich the grains. To prepare *couscous* for four people, put 1 lb pre-cooked *couscous* in a bowl, pour over about 1¼ cups boiling water, stir well and leave for ten minutes. Add another 1¼ cups water and two teaspoons olive oil and fork through the *couscous* to make sure the grains separate, then leave for ten minutes until swollen and tender but still separate. Put into a steamer and place, uncovered, over a saucepan of boiling water for ten minutes, or for about 20 minutes over a pot of gently cooking meat and vegetables. Fork through the *couscous* to separate the grains then turn on to a warm large serving plate. Dot with butter, add seasoning and stir. Form into a mound with a large well in the center into which to put the meat and vegetables.

HERBS these are limited to flat-leaved, Continental parsley and cilantro, which are regularly used fresh by the bunchful, and mint which is used less abundantly and usually dried.

OLIVE OIL many North African cooks use large amounts of oil – too much for most Western tastes. The oil not only adds flavor but binds together the ingredients and thickens dishes such as *tagines*. For the recipes in this book, the amounts of oil have been reduced to suit Western palates.

RAS EL HANOUT literally means "head of the shop" or "shopkeeper's choice." It is a warming old, complicated mixture of many powdered spices, roots, barks, and flowers. Sometimes there are as few as ten, often as many as 20 or 25, perhaps even more different ingredients. Ingredients and proportions vary from cook to cook, but *ras el hanout* is generally thought to contain such aphrodisiacs as cantharides (Spanish fly). A simplified recipe for a home-made version of *Ras el Hanout* is on page 118.

SMEN is a type of preserved clarified butter prepared in a way similar to Indian *ghee*; it may be flavored with wild herbs. It has quite a potent cheesy taste that takes a little getting used to, especially for eating on bread. In cooking, *smen* lends a characteristic flavor to *tagines, k'dras* and *couscous*. In some Fez and Berber households, *smen* is packed in glass jars and kept for years, gradually becoming darker and more pungent with time.

See page 120 for a homemade version of *smen*.

SPICES spices are the backbone of North African cooking. They are used with generosity but judiciousness and great skill add character to cooking and enhance the taste of other ingredients. Spices also stimulate the appetite by producing enticing aromas and color to food, and aid digestion.

The most popular, indeed essential, spices are cumin, paprika, saffron, ginger, cinnamon, cilantro, and cayenne. Because of the frequency with which the spices are used in North African kitchens they never have time to go stale and it is important when you are cooking these recipes to ensure that the spices you use are absolutely fresh.

WARKA this is a tissue-thin pastry. It is made by patting small balls of dough 18 or 20 times in succession in a series of concentric circles, overlapping the circles slightly, on a metal domed metal surface heated over a brazier. In this way a wide, circular sheet of extremely thin, lacy, delicate pastry is made. It takes practice, skill and patience to make, and nowadays is often bought ready-made from specialist shops. Filo pastry is the best alternative for Western cooks or, in some recipes, Chinese spring roll wrappers.

Wines of the Region

Many North Africans will not drink wine as they are governed by the rules of Islam, which forbid the consumption of alcohol. However, wine production, and consumption, pre-dates the arrival of Islam. The Romans introduced the vine to the area. It thrived in the favorable climate and soil conditions, and winemaking spread rapidly until the fall of the Roman Empire. Winemaking remained in decline until the French and Spanish began colonization and planted southern French and, to a lesser extent, Spanish grape varieties. When Morocco gained independence in 1956 the government instituted a quality control system based on the French Appellation Controlle system. Tunisia and Algeria soon followed suit. The area under vines again rapidly increased and in 1973 the wine industry was officially classified as a national industry in Morocco. But since then Islam has exercized its influence again and viticulture has declined. The vast majority of North African wines are bulk varieties, mainly red, for blending but some pleasant ones for local drinking can be found.

Variations on a Theme

Inevitably, when covering the cuisine of three similar, neighboring countries quite a number of dishes will cross national boundaries. However, each country puts its own stamp on a recipe, using slightly different methods and flavorings. Various versions of the same dish may also be met with in different regions, towns, villages, and even in different homes. Don't be surprised, therefore, if you come across a dish with the same name but which tastes different to the one I have given. You may also come across different spellings for the same recipe – names and spellings are a minefield in North Africa. Each country, and sometimes individual districts within a country, have their own version of Arabic. Furthermore, phonetic French or English spellings of North African dishes can present a problem. Moroccan Arabic, in contrast to classical Arabic, is a spoken language and therefore phonetic spellings vary enormously. For example, *b'stilla,* can also be spelt *bisteeya, bstila, pstilla,* and *pasteeya,* and the ultra-thin pastry used to make it can be spelt *warka* or *ouarka.*

ABOVE *Tiles above the familiar Tunisian blue of the door symbolising God's presence. Sidi Bon Said, Tunisia*

1

Soups

North African soups are spicy, substantial and nourishing, and are generally served as a supper dish. The most famous soup of all is the Moslem *Harira,* traditionally eaten at sundown during the month of Ramadan to break the day's fast, although it is eaten at other times of the year too.

Chunky Tunisian Fish Soup

BROUDOU BIL HOUT

There are clear similarities between this substantial fish soup and bouillabaisse, *which comes from the other side of the Mediterranean. Any selection of fish and shellfish can be used except oily fish such as mackerel and sardines. If you like, you can use the heads, tails, skin and bones to make fish broth for the soup.*

SERVES 6–8

3 tbsp olive oil

2 onions, chopped

3 garlic cloves, chopped

1 red pepper, chopped

about 1 tsp Harissa (see page 120)

¼ tsp crushed saffron threads

¼–½ tsp ground cinnamon

¼–½ tsp ground cumin

1 fennel bulb, diced, feathery fronds reserved

2 large potatoes, chopped

2½–3 tbsp lemon juice

6 cups fish broth or water

4½ lb mixed fish and shellfish, prepared

4 well-flavored tomatoes, peeled, deseeded and chopped

1 large bunch of mixed cilantro and parsley, finely chopped

salt and pepper

good bread, to serve

Heat the oil in a large saucepan, then fry the onion until softened but not colored. Add the garlic and red pepper, cook for 2–3 minutes then stir in the *Harissa*, spices, fennel, potatoes, lemon juice, and broth or water. Bring to the boil then simmer for about 20 minutes until the potatoes are almost cooked. Add the fish, tomatoes, herbs, seasoning, and water as necessary, and cook gently until the fish is tender. Serve sprinkled with the reserved fennel fronds and accompanied by good bread.

ABOVE *Fisher boats at Medique, Morocco*

Lentil Soup

For centuries lentils have provided a simple, adaptable, accessible and portable source of protein and calories; Arab cooks have been using them since the time of the ancient Sumerians and Egyptians.

SERVES 6–8

2 tbsp olive oil
1 red onion, finely chopped
2 garlic cloves, chopped
12 oz shin of veal, chopped
½ tsp each ground cumin
   and cinnamon
¼ tsp cayenne pepper
6 oz green lentils

6¼ cups water
3 small-to-medium carrots,
   diced
3 celery sticks, chopped
2 potatoes, diced
salt and pepper
1 bunch of cilantro,
   coarsely chopped
lemon juice

Boil the lentils in a pan of water for at least 10 minutes, drain, and set aside. Heat the oil in a pan, then cook the onion, garlic and veal, stirring frequently, until the onion is soft. Stir in the spices until fragrant, then add the lentils and water. Bring to the boil and skin the scum from the surface. Partly cover and simmer for about one hour until the meat is tender.

Add the vegetables and cook for a further 30–40 minutes. Season and stir in the cilantro, and lemon juice to taste. Serve straight away.

Chickpea Soup

LABLABI

Lablabi is a thick garlicky soup from Tunisia. It is usually extremely rich, but I have reduced the amount of oil here. The taste of all the garlic mellows with the long cooking. Add some ground spices, such as cumin, cilantro, and paprika if you like.

SERVES 4

6 tbsp olive oil
10 garlic cloves, crushed
12 oz chickpeas, soaked
   overnight and drained
10 cups water

1 red onion, finely chopped
2 carrots, chopped
1 head of celery, chopped
salt and pepper
lemon juice
1 bunch of cilantro,
   chopped

Heat 4 tbsps oil in a large pan, then cook the garlic until fragrant. Stir in the chickpeas then add the water and bring to the boil. Skim the scum from the surface, then simmer until the chickpeas are tender.

Meanwhile, heat the remaining oil in a flameproof earthenware casserole, add the onion, carrots and celery, cover and cook gently for about 20 minutes.

Add the vegetables to the beans, then purée half the mixture in a food processor or blender, or rub through a sieve. Stir back into the soup and reheat. Add seasoning and lemon juice to taste and sprinkle with cilantro.

LEFT *Lentil Soup*

Lamb and Vegetable Soup with Vermicelli

──── CHORBAH ────

*Variations of this thickened vermicelli soup are found throughout the Maghreb,
although the name may vary slightly. Traditionally, lamb in the Maghreb is
tough so the meat would be simmered in one piece, with the bones, for about one
hour first, to make sure it was sufficiently tender to eat. As our modern-day lamb
is more tender to start with, the cooking time has been reduced.*

SERVES 6

4 onions, chopped
3 garlic cloves, chopped
3 red peppers, chopped
1½ lb lean lamb, cubed
3 tbsp olive oil
2 lamb bones, cracked
8 cups broth or water
salt and pepper

pinch of crushed dried red
    chilies
4 tomatoes, chopped
½ cup dried apricots
1–1½ tbsp chopped mint
    leaves
½ cup vermicelli
1 tbsp lemon juice
chopped fresh parsley and
    mint, to garnish

Heat the oil in a large saucepan, then cook the
onions, garlic, peppers and lamb, stirring
occasionally, for about 10 minutes. Add the bones,
broth, seasoning, chili, tomatoes, apricots, and mint
and bring just to the boil then simmer for about 1¼–
1½ hours until the lamb is very tender.

Bring to the boil, add the vermicelli and cook for 5
minutes until tender. Pour the soup into a warmed
tureen, stir in the lemon juice and garnish with
chopped parsley and mint.

RIGHT *North Africa shows
the Middle Eastern influence
in its architecture*

Harira

*At sunset in Morocco during the month of Ramadan, a firing cannon signals the
end of the day's fast, and heralds the time to sit down to rich, red and spicy
Harira. Harira is not eaten only at Ramadan, however.
Chicken can be used instead of lamb and using chicken broth in place of water,
to make a lighter soup, or meat may be omitted altogether and another vegetable
or two, such as eggplant and zucchini, added to make a vegetarian soup.
The soup is sometimes thickened at the end of cooking with flour, or with eggs.*

SERVES 6

2 tbsp olive oil
8 oz lean lamb, cubed
1 onion, chopped
½ cup chickpeas, soaked
    overnight and drained
6¼ cups water
½ cup red lentils
salt and pepper

14 oz tomatoes, peeled,
    deseeded and chopped
1 tbsp tomato paste
1 tsp ground cinnamon
1 red bell pepper, deseeded
    and chopped
¼ cup vermicelli
1 bunch of cilantro,
    chopped
lemon wedges, to serve

Heat the oil in a large saucepan, then fry the lamb until lightly and evenly browned. Stir in the onion and cook gently until softened. Add the chickpeas and water, bring to the boil, then cover and simmer for 1 hour, or until the chickpeas are almost tender.

Add the lentils, tomatoes, tomato paste, cinnamon and red pepper and simmer for about 15 minutes. Then add the vermicelli, bring to the boil and simmer for a further 15 minutes, until the lentils and vermicelli are tender. Stir in the cilantro and seasoning. Serve with lemon wedges.

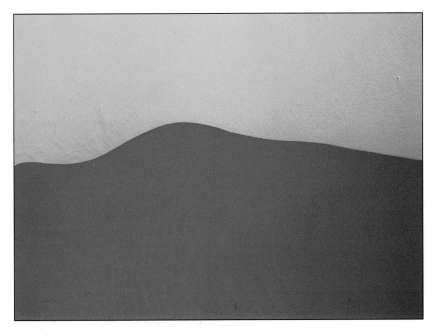

ABOVE *Light and shade contrast vividly in the Algerian desert*

Fish, Tomato, and Potato Soup

——————— SHORBA BIL HOUT ———————

Any white fish could be used for this Algerian soup, but I find that delicate or indeterminately flavored fish, such as plaice, sole and whiting, are overpowered by the other ingredients, but cod or haddock would be suitable. Although not traditional, I sometimes also include trout.

SERVES 6

3 tbsp olive oil
2 onions, chopped
4 garlic cloves, crushed
1 lb well-flavored tomatoes, peeled, deseeded and chopped
1½ tsp paprika pepper
pinch of cayenne pepper
good pinch of crushed saffron threads

2 bay leaves
1–1½ tsp fresh thyme
2 large potatoes, cubed
10 cups water
2¼ lb firm white fish fillets, skinned
2½–4 tbsp lemon juice
salt and pepper
2 eggs

Heat the oil in a large saucepan, then fry the onion until softened but not colored. Add the garlic and tomatoes and cook for about 10 minutes until the tomatoes have given up some of their liquid. Thoroughly stir in the paprika, cayenne, saffron, herbs, and potatoes then add the water and bring to the boil. Simmer for about 15 minutes until the potatoes are almost cooked. Then, add the fish and cook very gently until it flakes.

Discard the bay leaves and purée the soup in a blender or by rubbing through a sieve. Return to the pan and reheat, adding extra water if it is too thick – it will thicken slightly more when the eggs are added. Add lemon juice and seasoning to taste.

In a small bowl, beat the eggs with a ladleful of the soup. Over a low heat, stir the egg mix into the soup and heat gently, stirring, until thickened; do not allow to boil.

2

Appetizers, Snacks, and Salads

Quite a number of North African so-called salads are not salads as we know them, but dips or pastes. Others are made of a type of vegetable or combination of vegetables, and may be cooked or raw. You can serve a selection of salads as a first course, and then leave them on the table throughout the meal. They can also be served as snacks if accompanied by good bread.

Broiled Red Pepper and Tomato Salad

— SALADE DE POIVRONS ET TOMATOES —

Broiling the red peppers and tomatoes (which is traditionally done over a barbecue) gives them a delicious smoky taste and silky texture. This salad comes from Morocco and can be flavored with cumin and cayenne if you like, and thin strips or diced half of a preserved lemon. It can be served as a first course, or with broiled meats, poultry or fish.

SERVES 4

3 large red or green bell
   peppers
4 well-flavored tomatoes
2 garlic cloves, finely
   chopped

salt and pepper
1 small bunch of parsley,
   chopped, if liked

Preheat the broiler and place the peppers and tomatoes in a broiler pan then broil them, turning occasionally until evenly charred and blistered. Leave until cool enough to handle, then remove and discard the skins. Remove and discard the cores and seeds. Dice the flesh, place in a bowl, and mix together.

Sprinkle over the garlic, seasoning and parsley, cover and chill. Drain off any excess liquid before serving.

Broiled Red Pepper Salad with Eggs

— SALATAT MESHWIYA —

The capers and lemon juice give a bright piquancy to this brilliantly colored salad.

SERVES 4

4 red peppers, halved
2 tbsp lemon juice
4 tbsp olive oil
salt and pepper
4 well-flavored tomatoes,
   sliced

1 red onion, sliced
3 hard-boiled eggs
2 tsp capers
oil-cured black olives and
   chopped fresh parsley for
   garnish

Preheat the broiler, place the peppers in a broiler pan and cook, turning occasionally until charred and blistered. Leave until cool enough to handle then, holding each pepper-half in turn over a bowl to catch the juices, remove and discard the skin. Slice the peppers.

Add the lemon juice, oil and seasoning to the bowl and whisk together with the pepper juices.

Mix the peppers with the tomatoes, onion, eggs, and capers, pour over the dressing and sprinkle with olives and chopped parsley.

RIGHT *Broiled Red
Pepper and Tomato Salad*

Bulgar, Red Pepper, Cucumber, and Cheese Salad

*Oil-cured black olives can also be added to this salad just before serving,
if you like.*

SERVES 4–6

1½ cups bulgar wheat
1¼ cups boiling water
4 tbsp olive oil
3 tbsp lemon juice
2 tbsp chopped fresh mint
3 tbsp chopped fresh
   cilantro
salt and pepper

1 red bell pepper, grilled,
   peeled and sliced
1 bunch of plump scallions,
   chopped
2 garlic cloves, chopped
½ cucumber, coarsely
   chopped
2 cups feta cheese,
   crumbled
lime wedges, to serve

Place the bulgar wheat in a large bowl, add the boiling water and leave to soak for 30 minutes, stirring occasionally with a fork, until the water has been absorbed.

In a mixing bowl, whisk together the oil, lemon juice and seasoning. Pour oil mixture over the bulgar wheat, add the herbs and mix well. Then mix in the remaining ingredients. Cover and chill until required. Serve garnished with lime wedges.

Spiced Whole Carrot Salad

SERVES 4

1 lb small carrots
1 garlic clove
½ tsp paprika
½ tsp ground cumin
pinch each of ground
   cinnamon, cayenne, and
   sugar

3 tbsp lemon juice
2 tbsp fresh chopped
   parsley
1½ tbsp olive oil
salt

Cook the carrots and garlic in a pan of boiling salted water until just tender. Drain. Discard the garlic and slice the carrots. Place in a serving dish.

In a small bowl, mix together the spices, sugar and lemon juice, then pour over the carrots and toss together. Cover and chill.

Just before serving, sprinkle over the parsley and olive oil.

LEFT *Bulgar, Red Pepper,
Cucumber, and Cheese Salad*

Stuffed Fried Bread Parcels

—————— KHOBZ BISHEMAR ——————

Eaten hot, straight from the griddle or frying pan, these parcels make a delicious snack. Don't be put off by the thought of the beef suet – the yeast dough is pricked before cooking so it absorbs the excess fat from filling, making it rich and tasty. It is not so good cold.

SERVES 4

1 quantity Moroccan bread
 dough, kneaded (see
 page 110)
butter, for frying
salt

FOR THE FILLING:

scant ½ cup beef suet,
 finely chopped
1 dried red chili, finely
 chopped
3 tbsp finely chopped onion
3 tbsp finely chopped fresh
 parsley
½ tsp ground cumin
1 tsp paprika

With lightly oiled hands, form the dough into four balls then flatten each to a rectangle about 12 x 8 inches.

In a bowl, mix together the filling ingredients. Spread one quarter of the mixture along the center of each dough rectangle, then fold one long side over the filling. Fold over the other long side. Flatten each rectangle to 12 x 8 inches, then fold again as above. Transfer to a buttered baking sheet, cover and leave to rise.

Heat a griddle or heavy frying pan and add a small knob of butter. Using a fork, prick the dough parcels five or six times on each side. Fry the parcels for 8–10 minutes each side until crisp and golden. Serve hot, brushed lightly with extra melted butter, if liked.

RIGHT *The Sahara desert, Algeria*

Egg-filled Tunisian Fried Pastries

BRIKS A L'OEUF

*Serve these light crisp Tunisian pastries immediately they are cooked, and take
care that the egg does not trickle down your chin.
Although not authentic, Chinese spring roll wrappers make a useful alternative
to the traditional* warka *pastry, which may be hard to obtain.*

MAKES 4

¾ oz butter

3–4 scallions, finely
   chopped

1 tbsp chopped fresh
   parsley

4 oz canned tuna, drained
   and mashed

a few capers, chopped

1 tbsp freshly grated
   Parmesan cheese, if liked

salt and pepper

4 warka leaves or Chinese
   spring roll wrappers

4 small eggs

1 egg white, lightly beaten

oil for frying

lemon wedges, to serve

Melt the butter in a pan, then add the scallions and
gently cook until softened. Then mix in the parsley,
tuna, capers, cheese if used, and salt and pepper.
Leave to cool.

Spread out the *warka* leaves or spring roll
wrappers and place a quarter of the filling on one
half of each. Break an egg over each portion of
filling. Fold over the pastry or wrapper to cover the
filling and firmly seal the edges with egg white,
giving the edges a double fold for an extra firm seal.

Heat a 1 inch depth of oil in a large frying pan
until hot but not smoking. Slide in the *briks,* baste
the top with hot oil and fry until the undersides are
browned. Turn over and fry the other side.

Drain quickly on paper towels and serve with
lemon wedges.

Grated Carrot Salad

*A less piquant version of this spicy salad can be made by omitting the cinnamon,
ginger and honey, and adding 3 tbsp lemon juice, and sugar, orange-flower
water and salt to taste.*

SERVES 4

1 lb small carrots, coarsely
   grated

1–2 tbsp clear honey

juice of 1 lemon

5 tbsp olive oil

1 tsp ground cinnamon

½ tsp ground ginger

scant ½ cup raisins

salt and pepper

Put the grated carrot into a large bowl. In a small
bowl, mix together the remaining ingredients then
pour the mixture over the carrots and stir well. Leave
for 1 hour before serving.

Carrot Dip

OMI HOURIYA

This spicy homely Tunisian paste is served cold as a dip for bread. Although not traditional, I sometimes also serve it with broiled meats and poultry.

SERVES 4

1½ lb carrots chopped
2 garlic cloves, chopped
2 tbsp olive oil
½ small onion, very finely
   chopped

2 tsp ground cumin
1–2 tbsp lemon juice
about 1 tsp Harissa (see
   page 120)
salt

Cook the carrots and garlic in a pan of boiling water until the carrots are tender. Drain.

Meanwhile, heat the oil in a large pan, add the onion and cook until softened. Add the cumin and heat gently until fragrant. Add the carrots, garlic, and remaining ingredients to taste. Remove from the heat, mash together. Leave to cool.

Eggplant Dip

SALATAT ASWAD

---

*This delicious eggplant and tomato mixture is typical of the purée dishes which
are called salads in North Africa and the Middle East. Serve it as a dip with
oven-warmed pitta bread or sticks of crunchy vegetables such as celery and
cucumber. It also makes a tasty accompaniment to broiled meats,
poultry, and fish.*

SERVES 4

2 lb eggplant
2 garlic cloves, sliced
3 tomatoes, peeled,
    deseeded and chopped

1 tsp paprika
½ tsp ground cumin
1 tbsp chopped cilantro
1½ tbsp olive oil
3 tbsp lemon juice

LEFT Top *Pumpkin Dip,*
Middle *Eggplant Dip,*
Below *Carrot Dip*

Preheat the oven to 425°. Cut slits in the eggplants
and insert slices of garlic. Bake in the oven until the
skin is charred and blistered. Remove from the oven
and leave to cool.

Peel the eggplant, squeeze out and discard the
juices, then place in a bowl and mash with the
eggplant and garlic, tomatoes, paprika, cumin,
cilantro and salt.

Heat the oil in a frying pan, add the eggplant
mixture and fry, stirring frequently, until very thick;
this will take about 15 minutes. Pour off the excess
oil. Add lemon juice to the paste, to taste. Serve
warm or cool.

Pumpkin Dip

AJLOUKE ET POTIRON

---

*Tunisian Harissa and other spices transform pumpkin into a characterful dish
that is eaten cold with bread. Reserve the liquid from the pumpkin to use in
soups or casseroles.*

SERVES 4

1½ lb piece pumpkin
¾ tsp caraway seeds
¾ tsp ground coriander
1½ tbsp olive oil

1 plump garlic clove,
    crushed
about ¼ tsp Harissa (see
    page 120)
2–3 tbsp lemon juice
salt

Peel the pumpkin and remove the seeds and threads.
Chop the flesh and cook gently in a little water in a
covered pan until tender. Drain thoroughly.

In a large pan, gently heat the oil, add the caraway
seeds and coriander, stirring occasionally until
fragrant. Then add the pumpkin, garlic, *Harissa,*
lemon juice, and salt. Remove the pan from the heat,
mash all the ingredients together, then leave to cool.

Orange and Carrot Salad

The flavors of oranges and carrots have a natural affinity, each one enhancing the other. They are often combined in soup, but here they are used to make a tasty salad.

SERVES 4
1 lb carrots, peeled and
   coarsely grated
juice of 1 orange

juice of 1 lemon
1–2 tbsp orange-flower
   water
salt and powdered sugar

In a large bowl, mix together the carrots, orange and lemon juices and orange-flower water. Add salt and powdered sugar to taste. Cover and chill.

Parsley, Onion, and Lemon Salad

*This sharp, fresh-tasting Moroccan salad makes a good accompaniment to
broiled oily fish such as sardines, or it can be used, together with some olive oil,
to marinate the fish before cooking.*

SERVES 4

1–1½ bunches parsley,
  coarsely chopped
1 large red onion, thinly
  sliced

4 large lemons, preferably
  thin-skinned, peeled and
  diced
salt and pepper

In a large bowl, toss all the ingredients together, then
cover and chill lightly.

31

Tunisian Egg and Eggplant Tagine

TAGINE BETINJAL

In this dish, it is important not to cook the eggplant mixture after the eggs and cheese have been added otherwise they will become tough and the fat will seep unappetizingly out of the cheese.

SERVES 4
1 lb eggplant, diced
salt and pepper
oil for shallow frying
1 onion, coarsely chopped
2 garlic cloves, chopped
3 eggs, lightly beaten

1 hard-boiled egg, quite finely chopped
bunch of mixed cilantro and parsley, finely chopped
2 oz Gruyere cheese, grated

Sprinkle the eggplant with salt and leave to drain for 30–60 minutes. Rinse well under running cold water then dry on paper towels.

Heat a little oil in a *tagine* or heavy frying pan, add the onion and cook until soft. Add more oil. When it is hot add the eggplant until it is soft and lightly colored. Stir in the garlic and cook, stirring, until it becomes fragrant. Remove from the heat.

In a bowl, mix together the remaining ingredients, then stir into the eggplant mixture. Over a very low heat, cook gently for about 10 minutes until just set, then brown under a hot broiler, if liked.

ABOVE *Water pump and well at Kerzas, Tunisia*

Baked Eggplants with Cheese

BATINGAN BI JIBN

*Serve this appetizing Arab dish warm, as a first course or a light main course
accompanied by salad and pitta bread.*

SERVES 4

2 eggplants
2 tsp dried mint
2 tomatoes, peeled,
   deseeded and chopped
1 garlic clove, chopped
pepper
12 oz goat's cheese

Preheat the broiler. Place the eggplants in a grill pan, then broil them, turning regularly until the skin is charred and blistered. Preheat the oven to 400°.

When the eggplants are cool enough to handle, peel them and chop the flesh. Transfer to a bowl, then add the mint, tomatoes, garlic and pepper and mix together. Spoon the mixture into a baking dish and crumble the goat's cheese over the top. Bake for about 25 minutes, until the cheese is melted and lightly browned.

Cooked Vegetable Salad

SALADE DE ZAALOUK

*This salad from Tunisia is quite spicy-hot. It can be kept, covered, for 2–3 days
in the refrigerator; indeed, it tastes better if the flavors are given time to mature
and mellow.*

SERVES 4–6

3 tbsp olive oil
1 onion, chopped
4 zucchini, sliced
2 eggplants, cubed
2–3 garlic cloves, crushed
4 red peppers, sliced
2 fresh chilies, chopped
4 well-flavored tomatoes,
   peeled and chopped
salt and pepper
parsley or cilantro, to
   garnish, if liked

Heat the oil in a pan, then add the onion, zucchini, eggplants and garlic and cook for about 10 minutes. Add the peppers, chilies, and tomatoes, season and cook gently, stirring occasionally, until the vegetables are tender and there is no free liquid.

Transfer to a bowl and leave to cool. Garnish with parsley or cilantro, if liked.

Chicken Strips with Mint

These delicately marinated chicken strips are threaded onto skewers before being broiled or barbecued. Spearmint (the variety of mint most often used) is popular fresh and dried; usually it is home-dried in the hot sun then before using, the dried leaves are rubbed between the hands until the warmth releases the flavorsome essential oils.

SERVES 4

2 tbsp lemon juice

1½ tsp olive oil

2 tbsp chopped fresh mint, or 1 tbsp dried mint

2 garlic cloves, finely chopped

salt and pepper

14 oz skinless chicken breast, cut across the grain into ½ inch thick slices

lettuce leaves and tomato wedges, to garnish

In a large shallow dish, combine the lemon juice, olive oil, mint, garlic, and seasonings. Add the chicken, turn to coat with the lemon mixture, cover and leave for up to 2 hours in a cool larder, or up to 8 hours in the refrigerator. Bring into room temperature 30 minutes before cooking.

If using wooden skewers, soak 4 or 5, 6 inch skewers in water for 30 minutes. Thread the pieces of chicken onto the skewers, then cook under or on a preheated broiler, or barbecue for 2½–3½ minutes each side. Serve on a bed of lettuce, garnished with tomato wedges.

LEFT *El Djem, Tunisia*

34

Broiled Keftas

*It is generally recommended that the lamb used for Keftas should contain about
ten percent fat, to bind the ingredients together and keep them moist during
cooking. Leaner meat can be used, however, if you do not mind crumblier,
slightly drier Keftas.*

SERVES 4

1¼ lb lamb, freshly ground
1 onion, grated
1 tbsp paprika
1 tsp ground cumin
¼ tsp ground cinnamon
¼ tsp cayenne pepper
1 bunch of cilantro,
   chopped
several mint leaves,
   chopped
2 tbsp water
2 tbsp olive oil
1 egg, beaten
salt and pepper
salt and cumin, mixed, to
   serve

Mix all the ingredients together then knead well to make a homogenous paste; this may take 15 minutes. Chill for 1 hour.

Preheat the broiler or barbecue. Form the meat mixture into small cakes about 2 inches in diameter and ¾ inch thick. Broil or barbecue for a few minutes each side. Serve sprinkled with a mixture of salt and cumin.

Kebabs

*Kebabs are one of the most famous dishes of the Arab world. Lamb is almost
invariably used, and traditionally it is not interspersed with vegetables on the
skewer as this would affect the cooking of the meat. Instead of marinating the
raw lamb, the kebabs are sometimes sprinkled with spices after cooking.*

SERVES 4

1½ lb lean lamb, ground
chopped fresh parsley and
   lemon wedges, to serve

FOR THE MARINADE:

4 tbsp olive oil
1 tbsp lemon juice
1 onion, grated
1 garlic clove, finely
   chopped
1½ tsp ground cumin
1½ tsp cayenne pepper
2 tbsp finely chopped fresh
   parsley
salt and pepper

Mix together all the marinade ingredients. Thread the lamb onto skewers and lay in a shallow non-metallic dish. Pour over the marinade. Leave for at least 2 hours in a cool place, turning occasionally.

Preheat the broiler or barbecue. Broil or barbecue the kebabs, turning occasionally, for 4–7 minutes, depending on how well cooked you like the meat. Serve sprinkled with parsley and accompanied by lemon wedges.

LEFT *Broiled* Keftas

Fried Peppers with Capers and Garlic

The essential character of this pepper dish comes from the slightly charred taste of the peppers which are fried till their skins are scorched. The dish can be served hot as a vegetable accompaniment, or chilled as a first course.

SERVES 4-6

4 tbsp olive oil
1¾ lb red peppers, cut into strips

4 garlic cloves, sliced
1 tbsp salt-packed capers
2 tbsp white wine vinegar
salt and pepper

Heat the oil in a frying pan until it is quite hot, then fry the peppers, stirring frequently, until they are charred around the edges. Add the garlic and capers. Cook until they sizzle, then stir in the vinegar and seasoning; because of the salt in the capers little additional salt will be necessary.

Allow the vinegar to evaporate for a minute or so, then either serve immediately, or leave to cool, cover, chill and serve cold.

Beet Salad

If you buy ready-cooked beets, make sure they have not been preserved in vinegar.

SERVES 4-6

2 lb beets
¼ red onion, finely chopped
1 tbsp finely chopped parsley

2 tbsp lemon juice
6 tbsp olive oil
pinch of chili pepper
salt and pepper

Cook the unpeeled beets in a pan of boiling water until tender. Drain and remove the skins under cold running water. Dice the beets, place in a bowl, then mix with the onion and parsley.

In a small bowl, whisk together the lemon juice, oil, chili pepper, and seasoning. Pour over the vegetables, toss lightly, cover and chill.

RIGHT *Fried Peppers with Capers and Garlic*

Orange Salad

*Oranges in North Africa, especially Morocco, are wonderfully sweet and juicy.
They are used to make many different refreshing salads for serving at the
beginning of meals and at the end.*

SERVES 6–8

6 ripe oranges, peeled and
    thinly sliced horizontally
12 fresh dates, stoned and
    thinly sliced

12 blanched almonds,
    slivered
1–2 tbsp orange-flower
    water
ground cinnamon for
    sprinkling

Place the orange slices on a shallow serving plate.
Scatter over the dates and almonds and sprinkle over
orange-flower water. Finally, sprinkle with ground
cinnamon. Cover and chill lightly.

Broiled Red Pepper and Tomato Dip

—— SALATA MECHOUIA NABLIA ——

This roast vegetable salad comes from Nabeul, in Tunisia.

SERVES 4–6

1 lb large red peppers
1 fresh red chili
2–4 garlic cloves, unpeeled
3 well-flavored tomatoes
1 tbsp caraway seeds

2–3 tbsp olive oil
salt
quarters of hard-boiled
    egg, chunks of canned
    tuna fish and black
    olives, to serve

Preheat the broiler and place the peppers, chili, garlic
and tomatoes in a broiler pan and cook, turning
occasionally until the skins are charred and blistered,
and the garlic is soft. Leave to cool then peel the
vegetables. Discard the cores and seeds from the
peppers and chilli, and the seeds from the tomatoes.
Put all the vegetables into a blender or food
processor, or through a sieve.

In a frying pan, gently heat the caraway seeds and
oil until fragrant. Add to the blender or food
processor with the salt and whizz to a paste. Chill
before serving. Serve in a bowl with quarters of
hard-boiled eggs, chunks of canned tuna fish, and
black olives around it.

Eggs poached on Pepper and Tomato Ragout

CHACKOUKA

The inclusion of fiery-hot red chilies pinpoints this as a Tunisian dish.

SERVES 4

3 tbsp olive oil

1 large onion, thinly sliced

12 oz red bell peppers, sliced

1–2 fresh red chilies, deseeded and chopped

1½ lb well-flavored firm but ripe tomatoes, peeled, deseeded and chopped

salt and pepper

pinch of sugar, if liked

4 eggs

Heat the oil in a deep heavy frying or sauté pan, then cook the onion until softened and beginning to color. Add the peppers and chilies and cook, stirring occasionally, until almost soft. Stir in the tomatoes and cook for a further 8 minutes or so until all the vegetables are soft but not mushy. Add salt and pepper, and a little sugar, if necessary.

Make 4 deep depressions in the pepper mixture, break in the eggs, cover the pan and cook gently until the eggs are cooked as you like them, basting once or twice with the juices. Serve immediately.

Potato Omelette

MAACOUDA BIL BATATA

This herb-speckled omelette has similar ingredients to the Spanish tortilla *but the potatoes are mashed rather than sliced. Serve it as a substantial snack, or a light lunch accompanied by a green salad. It is good eaten cold as well as warm, and makes a wonderful picnic food.*

SERVES 4

12 oz potatoes, chopped

1 red onion, chopped

3 tbsp olive oil

2 garlic cloves, chopped

4 eggs

1 tsp Harissa (see page 120)

1 bunch of mixed cilantro and parsley, finely chopped

salt

Cook the potatoes in a pan of boiling water until tender. Meanwhile, heat 2 tbsp oil in a frying pan and fry the onion, until soft and lightly browned. Stir in the garlic and cook, stirring, until fragrant.

Drain the potatoes and return to the saucepan. Over a low heat, mash the potatoes, then stir in the onions and garlic. Remove from the heat.

In a mixing bowl, lightly whisk the eggs with the *Harissa,* herbs and salt. Gradually beat the egg mixture into the potatoes.

Heat the remaining oil in a large heavy frying pan, add the egg and potato mixture and cook over a very low heat until the bottom has set. Brown the top under a hot broiler.

41

Dried Lima Bean Dip

——— BYESAR ———

Byesar is close to the hearts of North Africans, and many crave it when they are abroad. Dried lima beans are the usual main ingredient but in Tangier split green peas and scallions may be used. In another variation, the beans are cooked with cabbage and flavored with paprika, cumin, garlic, and salt, while Tunisians add Harissa or paprika and a generous seasoning of cayenne. Buy skinned dried lima beans if possible. The customary way of eating Byesar is to sprinkle a piece of bread with the accompanying slices then scoop up the dip.

SERVES 4–6

8 oz skinned dried lima beans, soaked overnight and drained

3 garlic cloves

1 tsp cumin seeds

virgin olive oil

salt

Moroccan bread (see page 110) and a small bowl of mixed ground cumin, cayenne and salt, to serve

Cook the beans with the garlic and cumin in a saucepan, just covered by water for 1–2 hours (depending on the age and quality of the beans) until tender.

Drain the bean mixture reserving the liquid, then purée in a blender or by rubbing through a sieve, adding enough of the liquid and olive oil to make a smooth cream. Season with salt and transfer to an ovenproof dish.

Just before serving, warm in the oven with a little more oil trickled over the surface and sprinkled with *za'atar* or thyme, marjoram, or cilantro. Serve with Moroccan bread and a small bowl of mixed ground cumin, cayenne, and salt.

3
Fish

With its curved coastline, North Africa has access to many fishing grounds both in the Mediterranean Sea and the colder Atlantic Ocean. Tunisia lands the richest and most diverse catches because its coast has one of the Mediterranean's widest areas of continental shelf, which is where the fish flourish. The commonest catches are red mullet, seabass, bream, sardines, anchovies, hake and shrimp, but local specialties can be found along the coast, at Oulidia, in Morocco, for example, where you may find sea urchins, oysters, and mussels on the menu.

Baked Fish filled with Stuffed Dates

*Shad are traditionally used for this Moroccan dish, but any large freshwater
fish, such as carp, can be used. Alternatively, use seabass.*

SERVES 6

¾ cup water

2½ tbsp ground rice

scant cup blanched
   almonds, very finely
   chopped

ground ginger

1½–2 tsp sugar

½ oz butter

1 lb plump fresh dates,
   stoned

1 shad, carp or sea bass
   weighing about 4¼ lb,
   cleaned and scaled

½ onion, grated

¾ tsp ground cinnamon

Bring the water to boil in a small saucepan, pour in
the ground rice, stirring, and return to the boil for 30
seconds. Remove from the heat, cover and leave to
cool.

Preheat the oven to 325°. Reserve 2 tbsp of the
chopped almonds and mix the rest with the cooled
rice, ½ tsp ground ginger, 1½–2 tsp sugar, butter and
seasoning. Fill the dates with the almond mixture.

Rub the fish with seasoning and a little ground
ginger and fill with as many stuffed dates as
possible. Put the fish on a large piece of oiled foil
placed on a baking sheet and add any remaining
dates. Sprinkle with the onion. Fold up the foil,
sealing the edges firmly together. Bake for 15
minutes per pound. Increase the oven temperature
to the highest setting. Unwrap the foil around the
fish, sprinkle the fish and fruit with the reserved nuts
and the ground cinnamon, and put on the highest
oven shelf until crisp and brown.

ABOVE *Pulses and nuts stall, Marrakech, Morocco*

Crisp-fried Fish

HUT MAKALLI

Small crisply fried fish are popular street food in coastal areas. The egg coating makes a protective shield around the fish, keeping it moist, and the semolina gives a good crunchy outer "jacket." Sometimes very small fish are used, even smaller than whitebait, or anchovies, small sardines, sprats, or small lemon sole. Sometimes this dish is served with Chermoula *(see page 126). You will need a large frying pan and you will find it easiest to cook the fish in batches.*

SERVES 4

4 eggs
4 tbsp chopped fresh flat-leaved parsley
¼ tsp ground cumin
¼ tsp paprika
pinch of chili powder
salt and pepper
1 lb sprats or whitebait, according to size, trimmed

fine semolina for coating
olive oil for medium-deep frying
lemon wedges and sprigs of flat-leaved parsley, to serve

In a mixing bowl, lightly whisk together the eggs, parsley, spices, chili, and seasoning. Season the fish, then dip in the egg mixture to coat evenly. Roll the fish lightly but evenly in semolina. Repeat the egg and semolina coatings once more.

Heat about 1 inch of oil in a large frying pan. When very hot, add fish in a single layer and not touching each other. Fry quickly until crisp and golden.

Drain immediately on paper towels and serve with parsley sprigs and lemon wedges.

Fried Fish

A tasty yet very simple Moroccan recipe for fried fish steaks.

SERVES 4

4 tbsp finely chopped fresh cilantro
½ red chili, deseeded and finely chopped
3 garlic cloves, finely chopped
½ tsp ground cumin

½ tsp black pepper
juice of 1 lemon
salt
⅔ cup olive oil
2–4½ lb fish, cut into 1½ inch steaks
semolina for coating

Mix together the cilantro, chili, garlic, spices, lemon juice, a pinch of salt, and half the oil. Rub into the fish, cover and leave in a cool place for 1–2 hours.

Toss the fish in semolina to coat thoroughly but evenly. Heat the remaining oil in a large frying pan, then fry the fish in batches until golden on both sides. Serve immediately.

RIGHT *Crisp-fried Fish*

La Gaulette Broiled Sardines with Tomato Relish

*Around the square at La Gaulette – a little town whose name means bottleneck,
because it sits at the neck of the ship canal connecting Tunis with the sea – there
is a cluster of restaurants specializing in fish. In summer, the tables spill far out
over the pavement and the smell of a busy charcoal broiler scents the atmosphere.*

SERVES 4

16 fresh sardines
sprigs of cilantro for
   garnish

FOR THE MARINADE:

1 garlic clove
2 tsp coriander seeds,
   toasted
1 dried red chili, deseeded
   and crushed
finely grated rind and juice
   of 1 lime
4 tbsp virgin olive oil
salt and pepper

FOR THE RELISH:

4 scallions, white part only,
   chopped
juice of 1 lime
8 oz well-flavored
   tomatoes, peeled,
   deseeded and chopped
1 sun-dried tomato half,
   chopped
1/2 dried red chili, deseeded
   and chopped
3 tbsp chopped cilantro

Using the back of a knife, scrape off the scales from the sardines working from tail-end to head. Using scissors, cut off the fins and cut along the stomach. Remove and discard the intestines. Wash the fish thoroughly and pat dry with paper towels. Lay the sardines in a shallow non-metallic dish.

Pound the garlic and coriander with a pinch of salt and the crushed chilli. Add the lime rind and juice, then gradually work in the oil. Pour over the sardines, turn to coat with the mixture, then cover and leave for about 1 hour in a cool place, turning two or three times. Mix the relish ingredients together in a food processor or blender.

Lift the sardines from the dish, reserving the spice mixture. Cook the sardines in a broiler pan under a preheated broiler for 2–3 minutes a side, basting with the marinade. Serve garnished with lime slices.

Algerian Broiled Sardines with Lemon and Coriander

This particular recipe comes from an ex-patriot Algerian living in France.

SERVES 4

6 tbsp olive oil
3 tbsp lemon juice
2 tbsp chopped fresh
   cilantro
good pinch of paprika

good pinch of cumin
salt and pepper
2 lb prepared fresh
   sardines (see above for
   cleaning sardines)

LEFT *La Gaulette Broiled
Sardines with Tomato Relish*

Mix together the oil, lemon juice, cilantro, and seasoning. Lay the sardines in a single layer in a large, shallow dish and pour over the oil mixture. Leave in a cool place for 1 hour, turning the sardines 2 or 3 times.

Preheat the broiler. Broil the sardines for 2–3 minutes a side, brushing with the lemon mixture as the fish browns and when turning them. Serve with any remaining lemon mixture poured over.

Bream with Preserved Lemons in Oil

DAURADE AUX CITRONS CONFITS

Daurade is the gilt-head bream, which is considered the star of the sea bream family, but if you are unable to find it use dentex or common sea bream for this Algerian dish.

SERVES 4

16–20 slices Lemons Preserved in Oil (see page 124)

1 bream, preferably gilt-head, weighing about 3¼ lb, or other firm white fish, cleaned and scaled

⅔ cup oil from the jar of lemons

1 tbsp chopped fresh cilantro

1 tbsp paprika

salt and pepper

Lay about 12 lemon slices in the bottom of a large shallow baking dish. Make several slashes along each side of the fish, season inside and out, put the cilantro inside and rub the outside with paprika. Put the fish on the Preserved Lemon slices and cover with more lemon slices.

Pour over the oil and bake the fish in an oven preheated to its hottest setting for about 5 minutes. Baste the fish, lower the oven temperature to about 350° and bake for a further 40 minutes or so, basting occasionally.

Tunisian Broiled Shrimp

Cooking this dish evokes memories of the evening sky in the sleepy Tunisian fishing village of Bizerta, the sounds of night drawing in, and the exotic aroma of charcoal broiled shrimp wafting tantalizingly past my nose.

SERVES 4

1 lb raw shrimp in the shell
2 garlic cloves, crushed
4 tbsp olive oil
1 tsp ground cumin
½ tsp ground ginger

1 tsp paprika
¼ tsp cayenne pepper
the leaves from 1 bunch of
  cilantro, finely chopped
salt
lemon wedges, to serve

Remove the heads and legs from the shrimp. Using kitchen scissors, cut the shrimp in half lengthways, leaving the tails intact. Lay the shrimp in a single layer in a large, shallow dish.

In a small bowl, mix together the remaining ingredients, except the lemon wedges, then pour the spice mixture over the shrimp and leave in a cool place for 1–2 hours, turning the shrimp occasionally.

Preheat the broiler. Broil the shrimp for 3–4 minutes until they turn pink, brushing with any remaining marinade as they cook. Serve with lemon wedges.

Almond Coated Baked Fish

—————— HUT BENOUA ——————

The Moroccan fishing port of Safi is the home of this unusual but delicious fish
dish with its crisp sweet, spiced coating.

SERVES 4

1½ cups blanched
  almonds, toasted and
  ground
½ cup powdered sugar
1 tbsp orange-flower water
1 tbsp ground cinnamon
½ cup water
¼ cup butter, softened,
  plus extra for buttering

salt and pepper
1 seabass or bream
  weighing about 4 lb,
  cleaned
1 onion, finely chopped
pinch of saffron threads,
  crushed

Preheat the oven to 375°. Put the almonds, powdered sugar, orange-flower water, cinnamon, 3 tbsp water, half the butter, and seasoning in a bowl and mix to a smooth paste. Season the fish inside and out then fill with half the almond mixture.

Mix the onion, saffron and remaining water together and pour into a large buttered baking dish. Put the fish on the onion mixture and spread the remaining almond mixture over the fish. Melt the remaining butter and trickle over the almond mixture.

Bake for about 45 minutes until the fish is cooked and the almond topping has a crust on it yet is still soft underneath.

Marinated Fish cooked in Spiced Oil

—————— POISSON EN TAJINE MQUALLI ——————

Halibut can be replaced by hake, cod or gray mullet in this recipe.

SERVES 4–6

2 lb halibut steaks
¾ cup olive oil
1 tsp ground ginger
pinch of saffron threads,
  crushed
stoned black olives and
  lemon quarters, to
  garnish

FOR THE MARINADE:

3 garlic cloves
salt
1 tsp cayenne pepper
1 tsp ground coriander
1 tsp cumin

To make the marinade, crush the garlic with a large pinch of salt then mix with the spices. Rub each halibut with the marinade then put in a single layer in a heavy baking dish and leave in a cool place for 6 hours. Preheat the oven to 375°.

Mix the oil with the saffron and ginger. Pour over the fish, cover and bake for about 20–25 minutes until the fish flakes easily. Serve garnished with olives and lemons.

RIGHT *Almond Coated*
Baked Fish

Small Fish Balls with Tomato Sauce

COUIRAT EL HOUT

*Fish balls are a favorite dish all along the coast of North Africa. The fish used
varies according to what is available. Sometimes the balls are fried, sometimes,
as in this Algerian recipe, they are cooked in a sauce.*

SERVES 4–6

2 slices of bread, crusts
removed, presoaked in a
little water
1½ lb fillet of firm white
fish such as hake,
haddock, or cod, skinned
and minced
1 large egg, lightly
whisked
1 bunch of parsley,
chopped
salt and pepper

FOR THE SAUCE:
1 red onion finely chopped

3 tbsp olive oil
2 garlic cloves, finely
chopped
3 large well-flavored
tomatoes, peeled,
deseeded, and chopped
½ red bell pepper, finely
chopped
1 tsp each ground cumin
and paprika
pinch of cayenne pepper
1¼ cups water
salt and pepper
chopped flat-leaved
parsley or cilantro, to
garnish

Squeeze the bread dry, place in a large mixing bowl,
add the other ingredients and seasoning and mix
thoroughly. With wet hands, form into balls about
the size of walnuts.

To make the sauce, heat the oil in a frying pan,
then add the onion and cook until softened. Add the
garlic and red bell pepper, cook for 2–3 minutes then
stir in the spices followed by the tomatoes and
water. Bring to the boil. Skim the froth from the
surface, add the fish balls and simmer gently for
about 8 minutes, turning once.

Transfer the fish balls to a warm serving dish and
keep warm. Boil the sauce hard until lightly
thickened. Pour over the fish balls and sprinkle with
chopped parsley or cilantro.

ABOVE *Coastline at Medique, Morocco*

Fish Tagine with Chermoula

There are many different versions of this dish, so feel free to change the ingredients given here to suit your taste.

SERVES 4

1½ lb grey mullet, bream or monkfish fillets

FOR THE MARINADE:

3 tbsp olive oil
3 garlic cloves, crushed
1½ tsp ground cumin
1 tsp paprika

1 fresh green chili, finely chopped
1 handful of fresh cilantro leaves, finely chopped
4 tbsp lemon juice
salt
lemon wedges, to serve

Place the fish in a shallow non-metallic dish. Mix together the marinade ingredients in a small bowl, then pour over the fish, cover and leave in a cool place 3–4 hours, turning occasionally.

Preheat the broiler, then place the fish in a broiler pan and broil for about 4 minutes each side, depending on the thickness, basting with the cilantro mixture occasionally, until the flesh flakes when tested with the point of a sharp knife. Serve warm with lemon wedges.

Fish and Celery Tagine

HUT BIL KARFAS

Here, celery stalks serve the function of the bamboo canes in Fish Tagine *with* Olives, *as well as adding flavor to the fish and sauce.*

SERVES 4

1 lb celery stalks
2 garlic cloves
salt
2 tsp paprika
1 tsp ground cumin
pinch of saffron threads, toasted and crushed
pinch of cayenne pepper
2½ tbsp olive oil
3¼ lb firm white fish such as bream or bass, cleaned

lemon juice
12 oz well-flavored tomatoes, peeled, deseeded and chopped
½ Preserved Lemon in salt (see page 125), pulp removed if liked, the peel chopped
1 tsp chopped parsley

Mix the garlic, salt, spices, and oil in a spice grinder. With the point of a sharp knife, cut 4 diagonal slashes on each side of the fish. Rub the spice mixture into the cavity and on both sides of the fish, pressing well into the slashes. Lay the fish on a plate and spread over any remaining spice mixture. Leave in a cool place, but not the refrigerator, for 1 hour. Preheat the oven to 375°.

Cut the celery stalks in half lengthways, then cut across into 2 inch pieces. Arrange in a single layer in a large baking dish. Put the fish on the celery. Scrape any spice mixture off the plate and spread over the fish. Cover with the tomatoes, Preserved Lemon peel and parsley. Cover with foil and bake for 30 minutes. Uncover and bake for a further 15 minutes or so.

Red Mullet with Red Pepper and Mint Sauce

ROUGET AU POIVRE ROUGE

Mint gives an unusual flavor to the red pepper sauce which is poured over
these pretty and delicious little fish.

SERVES 4

1½–2 tbsp olive oil
4 red mullet, about 8 oz
  each, cleaned and scaled
salt and pepper
1 onion, finely chopped
2 garlic cloves, chopped

1 small red bell pepper,
  charred and skinned if
  liked, then deseeded and
  chopped
pinch of cayenne pepper
3–5 mint leaves
small sprig of thyme
2–3 tbsp lemon juice

Season the mullet then fry it in the olive oil for 4–5 minutes each side, until the flesh flakes easily. Drain on paper towels then transfer to a warm plate and keep warm. Add the onion, garlic and pepper to the pan and fry gently until the onion is soft and beginning to color. Stir in the cayenne pepper, thyme, mint, lemon juice and salt and boil until slightly reduced. Discard the thyme sprig, pour the sauce over the fish and serve immediately.

Fish Tagine with Lemons and Olives

HUT BIL ZEETOON

For this tagine, *bamboo canes are traditionally laid in a lattice pattern in the*
bottom of the dish to prevent the fish sticking, but when the dish is cooked in the
oven, it does not matter if the canes are omitted.

SERVES 4

1 quantity Chermoula 2
  (see page 126)
1 firm white fish weighing
  about 3¼ lb, cleaned

1½ cups cracked green
  olives
2 limes, peeled and sliced
3 tbsp olive oil, if liked
3 tbsp lime juice, if liked

Rub half the *Chermoula* into the skin and cavity of the fish. Leave in a cool place for 1 hour.

Blanch the olives in three separate changes of water, then drain well and mix with the remaining *Chermoula*. Preheat the oven to 400°.

If liked, make a lattice pattern with bamboo canes in the bottom of a baking dish large enough to hold the fish. Alternatively, oil the baking dish. Lay the fish in the dish, and cover with the lime slices then the olives. Pour the olive oil, if liked, and a little water around the fish, cover the dish with foil and bake for about 35 minutes. Uncover and bake for a further 10–15 minutes. Sprinkle with lime juice, if liked. Serve with the cooking juices spooned over.

LEFT *Red Mullet with Red*
Pepper and Mint Sauce

Fish Tagine with Peppers, Potatoes and Tomatoes

——— HUT TUNGERA ———

Hut tungera makes a flavorsome, substantial fish dish.

SERVES 4

1 quantity Chermoula 1
  or 2 (see pages 126)
*4 fish cutlets or steaks cut
  across the fish, total
  weight 2¼ lb*
2 potatoes, thinly sliced

3 tomatoes, sliced
2 red bell peppers, sliced
1 tbsp tomato paste
1 garlic clove, chopped
4 tbsp lemon juice
4 tbsp olive oil
5 tbsp water

Rub some of the *Chermoula* into the fish and leave in a cool place, but not the refrigerator, for 1 hour. Preheat the oven to 375°.

If liked, lay bamboo canes in a lattice pattern in the bottom of a baking dish. Alternatively, oil the baking dish. Place the fish in the dish and cover with the potatoes. Spread with a little *Chermoula,* then cover with the tomatoes and peppers.

Mix the remaining *Chermoula* with the tomato paste, garlic, lemon juice, oil and water. Pour over the fish, cover with foil and bake for 25 minutes. Uncover and bake for a further 10–15 minutes. Allow to cool slightly, and serve warm.

Fish Baked with Preserved Lemons, Eggs and Onions

*Spiced eggs may seem rather unusual stuffing for fish, but they are typically
Moroccan, and surprisingly delicious.*

SERVES 4

5 tbsp oil
*10 oz red onions, finely
  chopped*
¼ cup butter
2 eggs
*2 tbsp chopped fresh
  cilantro*
*pinch of saffron threads,
  toasted and crushed*

*1 Preserved Lemon in salt
  (see page 125), pulp
  removed, the peel thinly
  sliced*
salt and pepper
2¼ lb white fish fillets
*chopped fresh parsley, to
  garnish*

Preheat the oven to 375°. Heat 2 tbsp oil in a frying pan and cook the onion until soft and transparent. Meanwhile in another pan, melt half the butter and fry the eggs until almost set, then stir them like scrambled eggs until set.

Stir the eggs, cilantro, saffron, Preserved Lemon peel, and seasoning into the onion.

Lay half the fish fillets, skin-side down, in a large baking dish, season and cover with half the onion mixture. Cover with the remaining fish, skin side up, and then cover with the rest of the onion mixture. Pour over the oil and dot with the butter. Bake for about 35 minutes then place the dish under a hot broiler to brown the top. Sprinkle with parsley and serve.

4

Poultry

In lands where meat is in short supply, poultry often plays an important part in people's diet, especially in poorer households. The unimpressively scrawny appearance of many North African poultry usually belies their flavor; local cooks know that the best way to cook this kind of bird is to braise it slowly, until the flesh is coaxed to fall away from the bones. Pigeons are used in the great Moroccan pie, *b'stilla,* as well as in other traditional North African dishes.

Chicken Tagine with Olives and Preserved Lemons

DJEJ EMSHMEL/DJEJ MQUALLI

The recipe cannot be made with fresh lemons – if it is, it will be an entirely different dish. The mellow flavor of the preserved lemons is beautifully complemented by pinky-brown Moroccan olives.

SERVES 4

2–3 tbsp olive oil

1 red onion, chopped finely

3 garlic cloves

salt and pepper

¾ tsp ground ginger

1½ tsp ground cinnamon

large pinch of saffron threads, toasted and crushed

1 chicken weighing about 3½ lb

3 cups chicken broth or water

½ cup greeny-brown Moroccan olives, rinsed (or Greek kalamata olives)

1 large bunch of cilantro, finely chopped

1 large bunch parsley, finely chopped

1 Preserved Lemon in salt (see page 125), flesh discarded if liked, rinsed and chopped

LEFT *Chicken Tagine with Olives and Preserved Lemons*

Heat the oil in a pan. Fry the onion until golden. Meanwhile, in a mortar, crush the garlic with a pinch of salt then work in the ginger, cinnamon, saffron, and a little pepper. Stir into the onions, cook until fragrant, then spread over the chicken.

Put the chicken in a heavy saucepan or flameproof casserole so it fits snugly, add the broth or water and bring just to simmering point. Cover and simmer very gently for about 1¼ hours, turning the chicken 2 or 3 times.

Add the olives, Preserved Lemon and herbs, cover again and cook for a further 15 minutes or so until the chicken is very tender. Taste the sauce – if the flavor needs to be more concentrated, transfer the chicken to a warm shallow serving dish, cover and keep warm, then reduce the cooking juices to a rich sauce. Tilt the pan and skim off surplus fat, if liked, then pour over the chicken.

Chicken with Grapes

DJEJ BIL EINAB

Squeezing the juice from fresh ginger is not a typically Moroccan practice but it adds a fresh note to this recipe.

SERVES 4

1½ in fresh ginger

1 tsp ground cinnamon

4 chicken portions

½ cup sweet butter

1 tbsp olive oil

8 oz green seedless grapes, halved

Squeeze the ginger in a garlic press to extract the juice, then mix with the cinnamon. Rub into the chicken and leave in a cool place for 2 hours.

Heat the butter and oil in a frying pan, then cook the chicken until evenly browned. Add the grapes, cover and cook gently, turning the chicken occasionally, until it is tender.

Chicken Stuffed with Couscous, with Spiced Honey Sauce

―――――――――― DJEJ M'AHMAR ――――――――――

This meltingly tender chicken with its almondy couscous *stuffing and spiced honey sauce, is served at feasts and celebrations in Morocco. Even though the sauce contains honey, traditionally the stuffing is sweetened with generous amounts of sugar. If you would like to try sweetened stuffing, I suggest starting with a 1–1½ tbsp sugar to see if you like it. Stuffing that will not go into the bird can be put heated in the top part of a* couscousier *or colander put over the saucepan towards the end of cooking.*

SERVES 4

1 large chicken

1½ red onions, finely
   chopped

3 tbsp oil

2 garlic cloves, chopped

2 tsp ground cinnamon

½ tsp saffron threads,
   crushed

¼–½ tsp ground ginger

salt

about 2½ cups water

about 2 tbsp clear honey

FOR THE STUFFING:

about 2½ cups water

2¼ cups pre-cooked
   couscous *(see page 11)*

3 tbsp raisins

½ cup blanched almonds,
   toasted and chopped

1½ tbsp orange-flower
   water

2 tbsp oil

1 tsp cinnamon

pinch of ground cloves

pinch of freshly grated
   nutmeg

salt and pepper

Stir the water into the *couscous* and leave for 5 minutes, stirring occasionally, until the water has been absorbed. Stir in the remaining ingredients.

Loosely fill the cavity of the chicken with some of the stuffing and pack some more in the neck end. Fold over the neck flap and secure with string or a skewer. Tie up the cavity with string. Heat the oil in a saucepan just large enough to hold the chicken, then gently cook the onions until softened. Stir in the garlic, spices and salt, then add the chicken to the pan. Pour in the water, cover, bring to the boil then poach for about 30 minutes. Add the honey and continue to cook for a further 45–60 minutes or until the chicken is very tender.

Remove the chicken to a warm serving plate. Taste the sauce and boil if necessary to concentrate the flavor. Spoon any separate stuffing onto the plate and pour the sauce over the bird and stuffing.

Chicken with Chickpeas, Lemon, and Parsley

—— SFERIA ——

*In this Algerian dish the sauce is thickened with grated onion, parsley and
cilantro, and flavored with saffron and lemon juice.*

SERVES 4

2 garlic cloves, crushed
salt and pepper
½ tsp ground ginger
pinch of saffron threads
¼ cup softened unsalted
    butter
1 chicken weighing about
    3¼ lb
1 cinnamon stick

1 small bunch mixed
    parsley and cilantro,
    finely chopped
3 oz green onions, white
    part only, chopped
6 oz chickpeas, soaked
    overnight
1 small red onion, finely
    chopped
lemon juice

Crush the garlic with a pinch of salt then mix it with the ginger, pepper, and saffron in a small bowl. Blend in half the butter then rub over the chicken. Put in a large dish, cover and leave in a cool place overnight.

Put the chicken and any juices left in the dish in a saucepan that will just fit the chicken. Add half of the herbs, the green onions, the cinnamon stick and chickpeas and enough water to just cover. Heat to simmering point, then cook gently for about 1¼–1½ hours until tender, turning the chicken a couple of times.

Meanwhile, melt the remaining butter in a small pan, then add the red onion and cook until softened, without allowing it to color. Lift the chicken from the pan, draining the liquid from the cavity back into the pan, and keep the chicken warm.

Add the onion and most of the remaining herbs to the cooking liquor and simmer until the liquid is reduced to a sauce. Add lemon juice to taste. Discard the cinnamon.

Joint the chicken and pile the joints on a warm deep serving plate. Pour over the chunky sauce and sprinkle with the remaining parsley and cilantro.

Chicken Tagine with Tomatoes

DJEJ MATISHA MESLA

Fragrant honey added at the end gives distinctive flavor and depending on the quality of the tomatoes, you may like to add some lemon juice just to lift the flavor.

SERVES 4

1 chicken, weighing about 3½ lb, jointed
3¼ lb well-flavored tomatoes, peeled and chopped
1 red onion, grated
1 garlic clove, crushed
pinch of crushed saffron threads

2 tsp ground cinnamon
¼ tsp ground ginger
⅓ cup unsalted butter or oil
salt and pepper
2 tbsp fragrant honey
toasted blanched almonds and sesame seeds, to garnish

Put all the ingredients except the honey and garnish, in a large, heavy flameproof casserole. Heat just to simmering point then cover and cook gently for about 1 hour until the chicken is extremely tender.

Remove the chicken and keep warm. Boil the cooking juices, stirring frequently, until well reduced and beginning to caramelize around the edges. Over a low heat stir in the honey then return the chicken to the casserole and turn to coat in the sauce. Serve with the almonds and sesame seeds sprinkled over.

Twice-cooked Chicken with Fragrant Sauce

—— DJEJ MAHAMMER ——

The chicken in this Rabat version of a Moroccan dish, is first pot roasted with plenty of onion and aromatic spices, then browned in butter. The pot roasting liquid is reduced to make a sauce for serving with the chicken.

SERVES 6

2 chickens, each weighing
   about 3 lb
2 red onions, finely
   chopped
2 garlic cloves, finely
   chopped
pinch of saffron threads,
   crushed

scant ½ tsp ground ginger
½ tsp freshly ground black
   pepper
salt
1¼ cups water
¾ cup olive oil
½ cup sweet butter

Put the chicken in a large saucepan with the remaining ingredients except the oil and butter. Cover, bring just to simmering point, skim the scum from the surface then simmer very gently for 1–1¼ hours, turning the chicken occasionally and adding a little hot water, if necessary. Lift the chicken from the pan, tilting so the liquid in the cavity flows out.

Heat the oil and butter in a large frying pan, add the chicken and fry until golden. Meanwhile, boil the liquid in the saucepan until thickened to a sauce. Serve the sauce with the chicken.

Pigeon with Oranges

Pigeon cotes are a common sight in rural and urban areas of North Africa. These birds are small and tender, more like our farm-reared pigeons than wild ones.

SERVES 6

3 tbsp olive oil

6 young pigeons

8 oz button onions, peeled

1 cinnamon stick

1 bay leaf

¾–1 tsp grated fresh
 ginger

large pinch saffron threads,
 toasted and crushed

3¾ cups chicken broth

salt and pepper

2 tbsp clear honey

2 oranges, peeled and
 thickly sliced

lightly toasted almond
 halves, to garnish

Heat the oil in a large, heavy, flameproof casserole, add the pigeons in batches and cook until browned. Using a slotted spoon, transfer to a dish. Stir the onions into the casserole and sauté until golden. Stir in the cinnamon, bay leaf, ginger, saffron, broth, and seasoning and bring to the boil. Return the pigeons to the casserole with any juices that have collected in the dish, cover and cook gently for about 1 hour, depending on their age, turning the pigeons occasionally, until they start to be tender.

Add the honey, cover again then cook for a further 30–45 minutes until the pigeons are very tender. Using a slotted spoon, transfer the pigeons to a large warmed serving plate, cover and keep warm.

Boil the cooking liquid until lightly thickened, adding the orange slices towards the end. Discard the cinnamon and bay leaf, if liked. Pour the liquid over the pigeons and scatter over the almonds.

LEFT *Pigeon with Oranges*

Chicken Kdra with Almonds

—————— DJEJ BIL LOOZ ——————

A kdra is a particular kind of tagine. Almonds become beautifully tender during the long, slow simmering and lemon juice is added at the end to cut the richness.

SERVES 4

1 chicken weighing about
 3½ lb, jointed

1 red onion, thinly sliced

¾ cup blanched almonds

½ tsp ground cinnamon

pinch of crushed saffron
 threds

½ tsp ground ginger

¼ cup sweet butter

1 large bunch of parsley,
 finely chopped

squeeze of lemon juice

salt and pepper

Put all the ingredients, except the parsley and lemon juice, into a saucepan. Just cover with water, bring to simmering point then cover and cook gently for about 1 hour until the chicken is very tender and almost falling off the bones.

Transfer the chicken to a warm serving plate and keep warm. Boil the liquid to reduce to a sauce, adding the parsley, and lemon juice to taste just before the end of cooking.

Chicken with Prunes, Honey, and Cinnamon

—————— DJAL BIL BARGOUG WA ASSEL ——————

*In this Moroccan recipe the chicken is cooked with cinnamon, while the prunes
are cooked separately and made into a sauce with the cooking liquor.*

SERVES 4

2 tbsp olive oil

4 chicken portions

small piece of cinnamon
stick

3 well-flavored tomatoes,
peeled and chopped

2 cups chicken broth

salt and pepper

4 oz ready-to-eat prunes

1 tbsp clear honey

1 tbsp grated fresh ginger

¼ cup raisins

pinch of saffron threads,
crushed

⅔ cup water

toasted sesame seeds, to
garnish

Heat the oil in a pan, brown the chicken, then add the cinnamon, tomatoes, broth, and seasoning. Bring just to boiling point, then cover and simmer gently for 45 minutes, removing the lid towards the end.

Meanwhile, cook the prunes with the honey, ginger, raisins, and saffron in the liquid for about 15 minutes until tender. Transfer the chicken to a warm serving dish and keep warm.

Boil the cooking juices until reduced to ⅔ cup. Add to the prunes and heat together for a minute or so. Pour over the chicken and garnish with toasted sesame seeds.

Chicken Stuffed with Dried Fruit

*This Berber dish is a good example of the North African predilection for
combining meat and fruit. Stuff the neck cavity as well as the back cavity, which
must not be packed too tightly. Warm through left over stuffing and serve with
couscous.*

SERVES 4

5 tbsp olive oil

1 onion, chopped

¼ cup pine nuts or
almonds, chopped

1 cup mixed dried fruit –
apricots, apples, pears,
prunes, raisins, soaked,
drained, and chopped

salt and pepper

3¼ lb chicken

Preheat the oven to 325°. Heat 2 tbsp oil in a pan, then cook the onion until pale gold. Stir in the nuts and cook for 2–3 minutes, then add the dried fruits and seasoning. Leave to cool. Stuff the chicken with the dried-fruit mixture and truss the bird. Brown the chicken in the remaining oil in a large heavy flameproof casserole. Sprinkle with salt and pepper and put the chicken on one side. Cover the dish and cook in the oven for 1½ hours, turning the chicken every 30 minutes so it is breast uppermost for the last 30 minutes.

RIGHT *Chicken with
Prunes, Honey, and
Cinnamon*

Moroccan Pigeon (or Chicken) Pie

———— B'STILLA ————

B'stilla *is one of the great dishes of North Africa. It is served hot-to-the-touch as a first course. To eat it, the thumb and first two fingers of the right hand are plunged through the crust into the steaming filling and the size of morsel required is pulled out.*
In Morocco the crust is made of tissue-thin warka *but if you are not in Morocco, filo pastry is the most practical type to use, although it will not produce quite the same fine, crisp pie. Traditionally, the poultry portions are left whole but the pie is easier to eat if the bones are removed after cooking. This recipe, from Fez, is a fairly simple version.*

SERVES 8

2 young pigeons, or 1 medium chicken, jointed
2 red onions, grated
½ tsp ground ginger
½ tsp crushed saffron threads
2½ tsp ground cinnamon
oil
salt and pepper
2 bunches of cilantro, chopped

2 bunches of parsley, chopped
8 small eggs, beaten
10 sheets of filo pastry
¾ cup blanched almonds, coarsely chopped and toasted
powdered sugar (optional)
ground cinnamon and powdered sugar for sprinkling

Put the poultry in a large saucepan with the onions, ginger, saffron, ½ tsp cinnamon, 3 tbsp oil, and seasoning. Add just a little water, so the birds are pot roasted and not boiled. Cover and cook gently, turning the poultry occasionally until tender.

Remove the joints from the pan and leave until cool enough to handle. Discard the skin, and bone the joints, if liked. Add the cilantro and parsley to the pan and boil until reduced to a thick, dryish sauce. Over a very low heat, stir in the eggs to scramble them. Remove from the heat.

Preheat the oven to 375°. Thoroughly oil a metal baking tin about 13 inches diameter and 2 inches deep. Lay a sheet of filo pastry in the tin, fitting it in to the shape of the tin and allowing any loose edges to fall over the sides. Brush with oil. Repeat with four more sheets, brushing with oil, so the tin is completely covered.

Cover with the pigeon or chicken pieces, then the egg mixture. Cover with a small sheet of pastry and scatter over the almonds. Sprinkle with 2 tsp cinnamon, and a little powdered sugar, if liked. Fold overhanging edges of pastry over the almonds then cover with the remaining pastry, brushing each sheet with oil. Tuck the edges inside the tin and under the pie. Bake for about 45 minutes until crisp and golden. Sieve powdered sugar over the top and make a lattice with ground cinnamon. Serve hot.

5
Meats

Lamb is far and away the most popular meat in North Africa; Islam forbids pork, and goats are used for milk rather than meat. Whole baby lamb are sometimes roasted, as for the Berber *mechoui,* traditionally prepared for festivals and ceremonies in the desert but now also cooked in towns and cities. Also, cubes of lamb, often first marinated in *Chermoula,* are threaded on skewers and grilled over charcoal; but most common of all are the succulent slow-cooked lamb dishes, braised very gently in fragrant *tagines* until the meat becomes so tender it can be broken apart with bread.

Lamb Tagine with Fennel

TAGINE EL LAHM BESBAS

The flavors of fennel, lemon, and lamb make a delicious combination. In Morocco wild fennel is sometimes used, but cultivated fennel is just as effective in this dish.

SERVES 4–6

2½ lb lean shoulder of lamb, cut into 1½ in cubes
1 onion, grated
2 garlic cloves, crushed
2 tbsp chopped cilantro
pinch of crushed saffron threads
¾ tsp ground ginger
½ tsp freshly ground black pepper

1 cup water
3 fennel bulbs, thickly sliced
2 tbsp lemon juice
salt
1 Preserved Lemon in salt (see page 125), quartered, flesh discarded if liked, and rinsed
½ cup Kalamata olives

Mix the lamb, onion, garlic, cilantro, and spices together in a heavy, flameproof casserole. Pour over the water, bring just to simmering point then cover and cook gently for about 1¼ hours until the lamb is almost tender.

Add the fennel, lemon juice and salt, cover and cook for a further 20 minutes or so, until the lamb and fennel are tender. Transfer the lamb and fennel to a warm serving dish. Scatter over the Preserved Lemon and olives, cover and keep warm.

If necessary, boil the cooking juices to reduce and thicken. Pour over the lamb and fennel and serve.

Lamb Tagine with Chestnuts and Chickpeas

MARQUIT QUASTAL

This wonderfully fragrant stew is often made with dried chestnuts, because they are more practical in Tunisia, but the flavor is even better when fresh chestnuts are used.

SERVES 4

3 tbsp olive oil
1 onion, chopped
2 celery sticks, chopped
2 garlic cloves, crushed
¾ cup chickpeas, soaked overnight, then drained

1 lb lean lamb, cubed
1 tsp ground cinnamon
pepper
3 cups chestnuts, peeled
2 tbsp raisins
salt

Heat the oil in a heavy flameproof casserole then add the onion, celery, and garlic and cook until softened. Stir in the lamb and brown evenly, then add the chickpeas. Cover with water and bring to the boil, remove the scum from the surface with a slotted spoon. Add the cinnamon and a generous grinding of black pepper, but no salt, cover and cook gently for 1¼–1½ hours until the lamb and chickpeas are almost tender.

Add the chestnuts, raisins and salt to the casserole and cook for a further 15–20 minutes until all the ingredients are tender.

RIGHT *Lamb Tagine with Fennel*

Moroccan Lamb with Apricots

—————— SIKBADJ ——————

Tunisian apricots are darker, firmer and sharper tasting than those commonly available. The nearest equivalents can usually be found in healthfood shops or local food markets.
Eggplants are sometimes included in this recipe, and saffron-flavored rice makes a good accompaniment.

SERVES 4

1½ lb lean lamb, cubed
2 garlic cloves, crushed
5 tbsp orange juice
4 tbsp olive oil
1 tbsp chopped fresh cilantro
1 tbsp chopped fresh mint
1 tsp ground cumin
pinch of freshly grated nutmeg

1 onion, thinly sliced
½ cup dried apricots, soaked overnight just covered by water
¼ cup pitted dried dates, coarsely chopped
2 cups broth
salt and pepper
2 tbsp sesame seeds, to garnish

In a large non-metallic dish, mix the lamb with the garlic, orange juice, 2 tbsp olive oil, the herbs and spices. Cover and leave overnight in the refrigerator, stirring occasionally.

Heat the remaining oil in a flameproof casserole, then add the onion and cook gently, for 5 minutes. Remove and reserve.

Drain the lamb, reserving the marinade. Quickly brown the lamb in the casserole then add the reserved marinade, the apricots and soaking liquid, dates, broth, onion, and seasoning. Bring just to the boil, then cover and cook gently for about 1 hour until the lamb is very tender. Uncover towards the end of the cooking to allow some of the liquid to evaporate and thicken the sauce. Serve sprinkled with sesame seeds.

Lamb Tagine with Prunes

TAGINE BARROGOG BIS BASELA

When the Andalusian Moors left Spain after the reconquest, and settled in Fez and Tetouan, the cooking of northern Morocco experienced a renaissance. This recipe is typical of the festive meat and fruit dishes originating from that time. The sweetness of the prunes and honey is counterbalanced by the spices and generous seasoning with black pepper.

SERVES 6–8

3 tbsp olive oil
1 large onion, grated
2 garlic cloves, chopped
2 lb lean lamb, cut into
 large pieces
small bunch of parsley,
 finely chopped
2 tsp freshly ground black
 pepper
1 tsp ground ginger
½ tsp crushed saffron
 threads

scant 2 cup prunes, just
 covered by water and
 soaked overnight
2 tsp ground cinnamon
salt
1–3 tbsp orange-flower
 water, to taste
about 2 tbsp clear honey, to
 taste
toasted sesame seeds and
 pine nuts or chopped
 almonds, to garnish

Stir the oil, onion, garlic, lamb, parsley, pepper, and spices together in a heavy, flameproof casserole. Add the prune soaking liquid and enough water to just cover. Cover the casserole and cook gently for about 1 hour until the lamb is almost tender.

Add the prunes, cinnamon and salt, cover again and cook for a further 30 minutes. Stir in orange-flower water and honey to taste and cook for a few more minutes. Serve garnished with toasted sesame seeds and pine nuts or almonds.

Saffron-baked Lamb

AGNEAU AU FOUR

A rich and subtle Tunisian dish.

SERVES 6

2½ lb waxy potatoes,
 peeled
salt and pepper
pinch of saffron threads

3 lb leg of lamb, in steaks,
 or chopped
½ cup olive oil
juice of 1 lemon

Quarter the potatoes lengthways, put into a bowl with the saffron and just cover with salted water. Leave for 30 minutes.

Preheat the oven to 350°. Drain the potatoes and reserve 1¼ cups of the soaking liquid. Layer the potatoes and lamb in a baking dish, pouring over the oil and lemon juice, and seasoning as you go. Pour over the reserved saffron liquid, cover and bake for 1½ hours until the lamb is tender.

LEFT *Saffron-baked lamb*

Lamb Pot Roast with Herbs

T'DLLA

In the authentic way of the desert, the lamb is pot roasted by laying hot coals on the top of the tagine slaoui. *When the dish is eaten, bread is rubbed lightly over the lamb then dipped in the sauce (which would be much richer in butter or* smen *than in this version). A piece of meat is then removed from the joint with the fingers, or using a small piece of bread if the meat is very hot.*

SERVES 5-6

1 red onion, finely chopped
2 garlic cloves, finely chopped
½ tsp ground cinnamon
½ tsp cumin
½ tsp ginger
¼ tsp crushed toasted saffron threads
pinch of cayenne pepper
salt
5 tbsp olive oil
5 tbsp water
1 shoulder of lamb, about 4 lb
¼ cup butter, softened, plus more for browning, if liked
chopped cilantro, to serve (if liked)

Preheat the oven to 375°. Mix together the onion, garlic, spices, salt, oil and water. Put half the mixture in the bottom of a heavy flameproof casserole or baking tin, large enough to hold the lamb. Rub the remaining mixture into the lamb and put in the casserole or dish. Spread over the butter. Cook over a high heat until the lamb is brown.

Add just enough water to come halfway up the joint and heat until it comes to the boil. Cover with a lid or foil and cook in the oven for about 2 hours until the lamb is so tender it pulls easily from the bone. If liked, then remove the lid, baste with extra butter and brown lamb under a hot broiler until crisp and golden. Stir some chopped cilantro into the cooking juices, before serving.

Lamb with Coriander Marinade

——— LABAN IMMO ———

When translated, the name of this Arab dish means "his mother's milk," because the young lamb is marinated in ewe's milk yogurt, before cooking.

SERVES 4

2 garlic cloves

salt

1 dried red chili, seeded
    and chopped

½ in piece fresh ginger,
    chopped

1½ tbsp cilantro

1 tbsp coriander seeds,
    crushed

1½ tsp ground coriander

1 tsp ground cumin

1 tsp ground turmeric

1¼ cups Greek sheep's
    milk yogurt

1 tbsp lemon juice

1¼ lb lean lamb, cubed

sprigs of cilantro, to
    garnish

Crush the garlic with a pinch of salt in a pestle and mortar, or with the end of a rolling pin in a bowl. Add the chilli, ginger and cilantro and work to a paste. Mix in the ground spices then stir in the yogurt and lemon juice.

Put the lamb in a non-metallic bowl, pour over the yogurt mixture, stir to mix then cover and leave in a cool place for 2–8 hours.

Preheat the broiler or barbecue. Thread the lamb onto skewers and broil or barbecue, turning occasionally, until the meat is brown on the outside and pink in the center. Serve garnished with cilantro sprigs.

Lamb Tagine with Quinces

——— SAFARDJALIYA ———

Firm apples or pears can be substituted, but they do not have the same luscious fragrance.

SERVES 6–8

2 tbsp oil

1 large onion, chopped

2 lb lean lamb, cubed

1 tsp ground cinnamon

½ tsp ground ginger

½ tsp saffron threads,
    crushed

2 large, well-flavored
    tomatoes, peeled and
    chopped

1½ lb quinces

juice of ½ lemon

1 tbsp clear honey

salt and pepper

Heat the oil in a heavy flameproof casserole then add the onion and cook until tender. Add the meat, cook until evenly browned then stir in the spices for about 1 minute. Add the tomatoes and enough water to just cover. Cover the casserole and cook gently for about 1 hour until the lamb is tender.

Meanwhile, scrub the quinces. Cut into eighths, quarters or halves depending on size. Remove the cores and any blemishes, but not the peel as it adds flavor and a gelatinous quality to the casserole.

Add the quinces, lemon, honey and seasoning and cook for a further 15–30 minutes until the quinces are tender; take care that they do not fall apart.

RIGHT *Lamb with Coriander Marinade*

Lamb with Chickpeas and Apricots

──── MISHMISHEYA ────

Tunisians usually add sugar to this dish, but if the apricots are ripe and well-flavored you will probably find it sweet enough without adding any (although you might like to try sweetening it for an authentic taste).

SERVES 4–6

3 tbsp olive oil
1 red onion, chopped
1½ lb lean lamb, cubed
1 cup chickpeas, soaked
   overnight and drained

2–2½ tsp ground
   cinnamon
1¼ lb well-flavored ripe
   fresh apricots, halved
   and pitted
salt and pepper

Heat the oil in a large pan, then add the onion and fry until soft and golden. Stir in the meat, cook until evenly browned then add the chickpeas and enough water to cover. Bring just to the boil, skim the scum from the surface, then add the cinnamon. Simmer for about 1 hour until the lamb and chickpeas are almost tender. Add the apricots and seasoning and cook for about 20 minutes until all the chickpeas are cooked and the meat is very tender.

Spicy Sausages

──── MERGUEZ ────

Merguez make a tasty alternative to ordinary sausages, although some people may find them too spicy to eat for breakfast! They should be well flavored, so add more spices if necessary (to test the flavor, break off a small piece and fry to cook before tasting).

SERVES 4

12 oz beef, cubed
5 oz beef fat, cubed
1 tsp paprika
1 tsp mixed ground
   cinnamon and cloves,
   crumbled dried thyme
   and cayenne

salt and pepper
2–4 tbsp chilled water
sausage casings
1–2 garlic cloves, coarsely
   chopped

Pass the beef, fat and garlic through a hand grinder, then mix thoroughly with spices and seasonings; or mix the beef, fat, garlic, spices, and seasonings in a food processor. Add a little water to moisten.

Fill the casing with the meat mixture, tying into 2 inch sausages. Hang in an airy, warmish, dry place to dry for 24 hours.

Fry, broil or boil the sausages and eat hot or cold.

Honeyed Lamb

MROUZIA

In the days when refrigeration and freezing were uncommon, this rich, sweet Moroccan tagine was prepared after the celebration of the Aid el Kebir, the Feast of the Slaughter of the Lamb in order to preserve the meat. I have reduced the amount of honey in the recipe, but it is still quite a sweet dish, so I balance the flavor with lemon juice. Make the tagine 24 hours in advance (it will actually keep much longer) then reheat it gently when required. Because of its sweetness it is never served on its own but in combination with lighter dishes.

SERVES 6

½ cup butter
pinch of saffron threads
1 tsp freshly ground black pepper
1 tsp ground cinnamon
2 tsp Ras el hanout (see page 118)
salt

3 lb middle neck of lamb, with bone
1 cup raisins
3 onions, finely chopped
1 cup blanched almonds
⅔ cup water
1¼ cups clear honey
lemon juice

In a small bowl, crush the saffron with the remaining spices and a pinch of salt. Rub most of the mixture into the lamb and mix the remainder with the raisins.

Put the lamb and remaining ingredients, except the raisins, honey and lemon juice, in a pan, bring to the boil then cover and cook gently, stirring occasionally, for about 1–1¼ hours until the meat is almost tender; add more water if necessary to prevent the meat catching on the pan.

Stir in the raisins, honey and a good squeeze of lemon juice and cook, uncovered, for a further 30 minutes until almost all the liquid has evaporated, leaving a rich, thick sauce.

LEFT *Pack donkey, Hassi-Berkane, Morocco*

Spiced Lamb topped with Tomatoes

———— M'FKOUL ————

Cooked slowly under a blanket of well-browned onions, lamb shanks become wonderfully succulent and tender.

SERVES 6

1½ tsp ground cinnamon
¼ tsp ground cumin
¼ tsp ginger
1 small bunch of parsley, chopped
1 small bunch of cilantro, chopped
6 lamb shanks each weighing about 8 oz and 2 in thick

3 tbsp olive oil
1½ red onions, finely chopped
salt and pepper
1½ tbsp tomato paste
3 large, ripe well-flavored tomatoes, peeled, deseeded, and halved
fine granulated sugar

Mix together the cinnamon, cumin, ginger, parsley, and cilantro in a small bowl. Spread over the lamb and leave in a cool place for 3–4 hours.

Heat 2½ tbs oil in a heavy flameproof casserole, add the onion, sprinkle with salt and cook very gently, stirring occasionally, until browned and caramelized. Remove from the casserole. Preheat the oven to 325°.

Brown the lamb in the casserole, adding more oil as necessary. Add any remaining spice and herb mixture and seasoning then cover the lamb with the onions. Blend a little water with the tomato paste in a jug, then pour over the onions. Add sufficient water to almost cover, bring to just on simmering point then cover tightly and cook in the oven for about 1 hour 40 minutes until the lamb is tender.

Put a tomato half, cut side down, on each lamb shank. Check the seasoning and spicing of the cooking liquid, then baste the tomatoes. Sprinkle with fine granulated sugar, cover and return to the oven for 20 minutes.

ABOVE *Colorful spices and baskets shop in Essaouira, Morocco*

6

Vegetables

The inland areas of North Africa are too hot for cultivating vegetables, but in the fertile belt nearer the coast, however, vegetables thrive. As well as being served as side dishes with cooked meats, they are frequently combined with meat, poultry, grains or other vegetables in stews and served over mounds of *couscous*. North African vegetable dishes are often so good they can be served as a course in their own right, and are perfect for vegetarians.

Spiced Potato Cakes

These tasty fried potato cakes come from Algeria. The spicy mashed potato
mixture is also good served simply as it is.

SERVES 4–6

2 lb mashed potato
1 tbsp paprika pepper
2 tsp ground cumin
good pinch of cayenne
    pepper

1 bunch of cilantro,
    chopped
3 eggs
salt and pepper
oil for frying

In a large bowl, mix the potato with the spices, cilantro, eggs and seasoning. With floured hands, form the mixture into round flat cakes. Cover and chill for 30 minutes.

    Heat a shallow layer of oil in a frying pan, add the cakes in batches and fry until crisp and brown on both sides. Transfer to paper towels to drain. Serve hot.

Spiced Parsnips

MZOURA I

This version of Tunisian Mzoura is sweet and spicy, and made as hot as you
like with Harissa. I have also tasted it made, more traditionally, with carrots.

SERVES 4–6

2 lb small parsnips, sliced
3 tbsp olive oil
1 small onion, finely
    chopped
1 garlic clove, finely
    chopped
1 tsp Harissa (see
    page 120)

1 tsp ground cumin
1 tsp ground coriander
1 tsp clear honey
⅔ cup vegetable broth
salt and pepper
chopped cilantro, to
    garnish

Cook the parsnips in a saucepan of boiling water for about 7 minutes, then drain. Meanwhile, heat the oil in a frying pan, then add the onion and garlic and cook gently until softened. Stir in the *Harissa* and spices, then add the honey, broth, parsnips, and seasoning. Cook for 7–10 minutes, until the parsnips are tender and the liquid reduced to a sauce. Serve hot or cold sprinkled with cilantro.

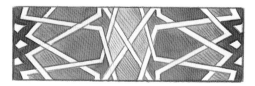

RIGHT Above *Spiced Parsnips* Below *Spiced Potato Cakes*

Cracked Barley and Broad Bean Couscous

CHEESHA SIKUK

Cracked barley, which is available from healthfood shops, makes a delicious, nutty-flavored couscous. *This recipe is from Morocco.*

SERVES 4

1 lb cracked barley
½ cup butter, diced
1 cup shelled small lima beans

2 plump scallions, sliced
salt and pepper

Rinse the barley under running cold water then leave to drain for 3 minutes. Butter the top container of a *couscousier* or a metal colander or steamer lined with muslin.

Squeeze the barley to expel excess water and put into the top part of the *couscousier,* rubbing the grains to separate them. Cover the container with muslin, then a lid, and put over the bottom part of a boiling *couscousier.* Steam for 20 minutes.

Tip the barley into a large roasting tin and break up lumps with a fork. Add ⅛ cup butter and very slowly pour in 1¾ cups water so the grains do not become soggy, forking through and stirring the barley to keep the grains separate. Leave to dry for 10 minutes before re-covering and placing back on the bottom part of the *couscousier.* Steam for a further 20 minutes.

Tip the barley into the roasting tin again, break up any lumps and leave for 15 minutes. Meanwhile, cook the beans and scallions in a small amount of boiling salted water until tender. Drain and stir into the barley with the remaining butter.

ABOVE *Low-level, flat-roofed houses, typical of North African dwellings*

90

Aromatic Chickpea Tagine

TAGINE BIL HUMMUS

In Morocco, chickpeas are sometimes peeled to make a more "refined" dish. The chickpeas are left in sunlight to soak, then drained and rubbed against the sides of a reed basket to remove their skins.

SERVES 4–6

2 lb chickpeas, soaked overnight and drained
4 tbsp olive oil
pinch of saffron threads, crushed
¼ tsp paprika
¼ tsp ground cumin
¼ tsp ginger
¼ tsp cinnamon

3 large well-flavored tomatoes, peeled, deseeded and chopped
1 red onion, coarsely grated
4 sprigs of cilantro, chopped
6 sprigs of parsley, chopped
salt, black pepper and chili pepper

Cook the chickpeas in boiling water until tender. Drain, and peel if liked.

Heat the oil in a large saucepan, stir in the saffron and other spices and cook until fragrant, then add the tomatoes, onion, cilantro, parsley, chickpeas, and seasoning. Cover and heat through gently for about 15 minutes, stirring occasionally.

Onion Tagine

MEZGALDI

Traditionally, the tagine is covered with a concave lid, and glowing coals are put into the lid so the onions cook from above as well as below. In modern homes with cookers, the oven and broiler are used.

SERVES 4–6

1 tsp ground ginger
1 tsp crushed black peppercorns
4 tbsp ground cinnamon
2 tbsp caster sugar
¼ tsp crushed saffron threads

salt
2 lb red onions, sliced
½ cup olive oil
2 celery stalks

In a small bowl, mix together the ginger, black peppercorns, half the cinnamon and sugar, the saffron, and salt. Place the onion slices and spice mixture in layers in a non-metallic bowl. Pour over the oil and leave for 2 hours.

Arrange the celery crossways in a *tagine* or heavy flameproof casserole. Add the onions and spice. In a small bowl, mix together the remaining sugar and cinnamon, then sprinkle over the onions. Cover and cook in an oven preheated to 325° for 40–50 minutes until the onions are meltingly tender. Brown under a hot broiler.

Couscous with Dried Apricots and Almonds

This quick, light, simple modern couscous *recipe was developed to suit the type of* couscous *now most widely available (see page 11). You can stir in butter or oil in the traditional way, or leave it out.*

SERVES 8

12 oz pre-cooked
   couscous *(see page 11)*
scant ¹⁄₂ cup ready-to-eat
   dried apricots, sliced into
   strips
salt and pepper

¹⁄₂ cup blanched almonds,
   lightly toasted
chopped fresh cilantro, to
   serve
sweet butter or olive oil, to
   serve, if liked

Put the *couscous* in a bowl and pour over 2¹⁄₂ cups water. Leave for about 30 minutes or until most of the water has been absorbed; stir frequently with a fork to keep the grains separate. Stir the apricots and seasoning into the *couscous* then tip into a *couscousier* or steamer or metal colander lined with muslin. Place over a saucepan of boiling water, cover tightly with foil and steam for about 20 minutes until hot. Stir in the almonds, cilantro, and butter or oil, if using.

Mixed Vegetable Tagine

The original recipe I was given for this tagine *contained scant ¹/₂ cup raisins, but I prefer the dish without them. You may like to add them when you make it — it's a matter of taste. Serve the* tagine *over* couscous *or rice.*

SERVES 4

³/₄ cup chickpeas, soaked
    overnight, then drained
    chopped
3 tbsp olive oil
4 small carrots, sliced
2 onions, chopped
3 garlic cloves, chopped
1 green pepper, sliced
2 zucchini, thickly sliced
1 tsp ground coriander

1 tsp ground cumin
3 tomatoes, chopped
2¹/₂ cups broth
salt and pepper
juice of 1 lemon
2 tbsp chopped fresh
    parsley, to garnish
4 green onions, white part
    only, finely chopped, to
    garnish

Cook the chickpeas in plenty of boiling water until tender; the time will depend on the age and variety of the chickpeas.

Meanwhile, heat the oil in a pan, add the carrot and fry until browned. Remove and reserve. Add the onion and garlic to the pan and cook gently until soft and golden. Add the pepper and zucchini and cook until softened. Stir in the spices and cook until fragrant, then add the tomatoes, carrots, broth and seasoning. Bring to the boil.

Drain the chickpeas, add to the vegetable mixture, cover and simmer for about 30 minutes until all the vegetables are tender. Stir in the lemon juice and sprinkle over the parsley and green onions.

Ladies Fingers and Tomato Tagine

———— MARAK MATISHA BIL MELOKHIAS ————

Be sure to choose small ladies fingers. In Tetuan, the ladies fingers are threaded on string, so they can be lifted out when the tagine is stirred. Served as a main course or with broiled or roast meats and poultry.

SERVES 4

1 lb fresh ladies fingers
3 tbsp olive oil
1 large onion, finely
  chopped
2 garlic cloves, finely
  chopped
1½ lb well-flavored
  tomatoes, peeled,
  deseeded, and chopped

pinch of paprika pepper
4 tbsp chopped fresh
  parsley
salt and pepper

Trim the stalk off the ladies fingers without cutting the pod. Heat the oil in a pan and fry the ladies fingers until lightly browned. Remove with a slotted spoon.

Add the onion and garlic to the pan and fry until soft but not browned. Stir in the paprika, stirring for 30 seconds, then add the tomatoes. Bring to the boil and simmer for 10 minutes. Add the ladies fingers, half the parsley, plenty of pepper and a little salt. Simmer, occasionally stirring, for about 30 minutes.

If the sauce is not well-reduced, transfer the ladies fingers to a warm dish and keep warm. Boil the sauce until thickened. Pour over the ladies fingers. Serve warm or cold, sprinkled with the remaining parsley.

Swiss Chard Tagine

———— MARAK SILK ————

There may appear to be too little liquid to cook the rice but the vegetables, especially the chard, give out a lot of moisture, too. The lid must fit really well so that no steam can escape (seal it with foil to be sure).

SERVES 4–6

2 lb Swiss chard
1 garlic clove, finely
  chopped
3 tbsp oil
1 tsp paprika

1 largish onion, finely
  chopped
⅛ cup long grain rice
4 tbsp chopped fresh
  cilantro
4 tbsp water
salt and pepper

RIGHT *Ladies Fingers and Tomato Tagine*

Separate the leaf part from the thick ribs of the chard. Shred the leaves coarsely and slice the stalks into ½ inch wide strips.

Warm the oil in a heavy flameproof casserole, add the chard stalks and the garlic, cover and cook gently for 10–15 minutes, stirring occasionally. Stir in the paprika, stirring for 30–60 seconds, then the onion, chard leaves, rice, cilantro, water, and seasoning. Cover with a very tight-fitting lid and cook, stirring occasionally, for about 30 minutes until the rice is tender; if necessary add some more water.

Spiced Glazed Carrots with Dill

—— MZOURA 2 ——

Dill, ginger and orange produce this distinctive version of Mzoura. Shake the pan towards the end of cooking to prevent the carrots from sticking.

SERVES 4

1 lb carrots, cut into thin
    sticks
¼ cup butter
1 tbsp sugar

½ in piece of fresh ginger,
    shredded
thickly grated rind of 1
    orange
salt and pepper
few sprigs of dill, chopped

Put the carrots, butter, sugar, ginger, orange rind, and seasoning in a pan and just cover with water. Bring to the boil then simmer for about 12 minutes until the carrots are tender and the liquid has evaporated.

7

Desserts, Pastries, and Breads

Sweet cakes and pastries are normally eaten with glasses of tea at any time of day, and are offered to guests and served by the trayful at special occasions such as festivals and family celebrations.

Bread is sacred in North Africa: according to a Moroccan story, a woman who defiled a loaf was imprisoned in the moon. Bread has to be treated with respect, and if a piece is seen lying on the ground it must be picked up, kissed and put somewhere so that it will not become dirty.

At dinner, it is customary for only one person to cut the flat, round loaves into wedges and distribute them around the table.

Almond Cookies

——— GHORIBA BIL LOZ ———

These rich, cracked almond cookies are a popular Arab sweetmeat. They are delicious served with coffee.

MAKES ABOUT 30
2 small eggs
1 1/3 cups powdered sugar,
   plus extra for coating
3 1/2 cups ground almonds

grated rind of 1/2 lemon
2 tsp baking powder
orange-flower or rose
   water, to taste

Preheat the oven to 350°. Oil a baking sheet. In a mixing bowl, beat 1 whole egg, 1 egg yolk and the sugar thoroughly together, then mix in the ground almonds, lemon rind, baking powder, and orange-flower or rose water to taste. Knead well with your hands to release the oil from the almonds, and add some of the remaining egg white if necessary to make a soft, workable paste.

Using oiled hands, roll walnut-sized pieces of almond mixture into egg-shaped balls.

Cover a plate with powdered sugar and flatten the balls on the powdered sugar. Place, spaced quite well apart, on the baking sheet and bake for about 15 minutes until golden.

LEFT *Almond Cookies*

Honeyed Almond Paste

——— AMALOU ———

This is a famous dish from the Souss region in southwest Morocco. Traditionally, it is made with highly flavored oil produced by pressing the nuts from argan trees – these are unique to the region and have a famed attraction for goats, who literally climb up into the branches to get at the acid, pungent-flavored nuts. Amalou is served with hot baked or fried bread or used as a filling for pancakes. Walnut oil makes a substitute for argan oil.

1 tbsp vegetable oil
1 1/2 cups blanched
   almonds

1/2 cups walnut oil
salt
4 tbsp thick honey

Heat a little vegetable oil in a pan, then add the almonds and brown. Drain on paper towels then process them in a blender with the walnut oil and salt until smooth and creamy. Add the honey and process briefly until well blended. Pour into a jar, cover and keep in the refrigerator. The paste should then keep for at least two months.

Fried Yeast Pastries

———————— RGHAIF ————————

The dough for these pastries is made in the same way as the dough for croissants or Danish pastries (but without the butter), rolled and folded to make it puffy and flaky.

SERVES 4

4 cups all-purpose flour
1 tbsp instant dried yeast
1 egg, beaten

about 1¼ cups water
oil for medium-deep frying
butter and honey, to serve

Stir together the flour and yeast in a mixing bowl, then slowly pour in enough water, stirring and then beating, to give a smooth, sticky, soft dough. Knead the dough thoroughly for about 20 minutes until it becomes firm and very elastic.

With oiled hands, divide the dough into 16–20 balls about the size of a prune. On an oiled surface and using oiled palms and fingers, pat and stretch each ball to a paper-thin rectangle about 10 x 9 inches; avoid tearing the dough and try to keep it evenly thin. Fold in the ends to meet at the center. Turn the dough halfway round, then repeat the folding. Pat out again to a rectangle about 4 x 6 inches.

Heat a ½ inch depth of oil in a frying pan. Slip in one *rghaif* and fry until it puffs up and becomes crisp and golden underneath, spooning over a little hot oil as it cooks. Turn the *rghaif* over and fry for about 1 minute. Serve hot with butter and honey.

RIGHT *Mosabite tomb in Taggit, Algeria*

Walnut and Almond Candies

——— FUSTUKH MAHCHI ———

*Walnuts sandwiched together with a rosewater flavored almond mixture make
a delicious way to end a meal Tunisian-style.*

MAKES 12

¾ cup ground almonds
1 tsp rose water
1 egg yolk
24 walnut halves

¾ cup sugar, plus extra for
　coating
⅔ cup water
1 tbsp lemon juice

Mix the ground almonds with the rose water, then add enough egg yolk to bind the ingredients together. Use the almond mixture to sandwich together the walnut halves.

Gently heat the sugar in the water and lemon juice, stirring until the sugar has dissolved. Raise the heat and boil until the syrup has reduced by half.

Using a spoon and fork, lower the walnuts into the syrup and turn over. Lift out and roll in sugar to coat evenly. Leave to dry overnight.

Sweet Almond and Seed Powder

——— SELLOU ———

*It is traditional to serve this at special celebrations, for guests to take a spoonful
or two as they are eating other candies.*

½ cup sesame seeds
½ cup chopped almonds
1 tbsp oil
½–1 tbsp anise seeds
1½ cups all-purpose flour

½ cup butter, chopped
¼ cup sugar
½ tsp powdered sugar
whole or slivered almonds
　and powdered sugar, to
　decorate

Scatter the sesame seeds in a broiler pan, toast under the broiler until golden and tip into a blender.

Mix the almonds with the oil in a broiler pan and toast under the broiler, stirring occasionally, until browned then add to the blender with the anise seeds and process until smooth.

Cook the flour in a large, heavy frying pan over a moderate heat, stirring constantly, until it has become golden brown. Remove from the heat. Melt the butter in a saucepan, stir in the flour and cook, stirring, until thick and caramel colored, but do not allow to burn. Remove from the heat and stir the seed and nut mixture, the sugars and cinnamon into the butter. Allow to cool. Serve decorated with almonds and lines of powdered sugar.

RIGHT *Walnut and Almond
Candies*

Gazelle's Horns

—————— KAAB EL GHZAL ——————

These popular curved, horn-shaped pastries, called tcharak *in Algeria, are
often known abroad by their French name,* cornes de gazelles *and variations
of them can be found in all the North African cuisines. If you prefer a more
delicate orange-flower water flavor in the pastry, use part water and part
orange-flower water to mix the dough.*

MAKES ABOUT 16
FOR THE FILLING:
*2 cups blanched almonds,
   ground*
⅓ cup caster sugar
½ tsp ground cinnamon
*about 2 tbsp orange-flower
   water*

FOR THE PASTRY:
1¾ cups all-purpose flour
pinch of salt
2 tbsp sunflower oil
*⅔–¾ cup orange-flower
   water*
*powdered sugar, for
   dusting*

Mix the filling ingredients together and knead to a
stiff paste; it will seem dry at first but will loosen up
and stick together as the warmth of your hands
releases the oil from the almonds. Set aside.

Preheat the oven to 350°. Oil a baking sheet. To
make the pastry, sift the flour and salt in a mixing
bowl and mix together with the oil. Stir in just
enough orange-flower water to bring it together as a
soft dough. Knead well until smooth and elastic.

On a lightly floured surface, roll out the dough
very thinly and cut into 3 inch wide strips. Roll
pieces of filling about the size of a walnut into thin
sausage shapes about 3 inches long and with
tapering ends. Place lengthways along the edge of
the strips of dough, about 1¼ inches apart.

Dampen the pastry edges with water and fold
over the pastry to cover the filling. Seal the edges.
Cut around the humps of filling with a pastry or
pasta cutter, or the point of a sharp knife and press
the cut edges together to seal.

Carefully curve the pastries into horn or crescent
shapes and put on the baking sheet. Bake for 20–25
minutes until lightly colored. Leave to cool on a wire
rack then dust with powdered sugar.

RIGHT *Hibiscus flowering in
Carthage, Tunisia*

Peach Salad

The ancient Persians brought peaches to North Africa, as well as melons and pomegranates. I like to eat this light, delicately-perfumed fruit salad on its own, but it can be served with crème fraîche, cream, thick yogurt, or icecream.

SERVES 4

4 large ripe peaches,
   peeled if liked, and sliced
about 3 tbsp sugar

2–4 tsp rose or orange-
   flower water
mint leaves, to decorate, if
   liked

Put the peach slices in a shallow serving dish, sprinkle over the sugar and rose or orange-flower water and mix together gently. Cover and chill for 2 hours. Just before serving, scatter over a few mint leaves, if liked.

Honeycomb Yeast Crepes

BEGHRIR

Like English crumpets, Beghrir are cooked on one side and bubbles burst on the surface to give a honeycomb effect. Butter and honey are, therefore, absorbed right into the pancakes. In Algeria, Beghrir are sometimes made from semolina.

SERVES 4–6

4 cups all-purpose flour
1 tbsp instant dried yeast
1 egg, beaten
about 1½ cups water, or
   mixed water and milk

melted butter, and warm
   honey flavored with
   orange-flower water, to
   serve

Stir together the flour and yeast in a mixing bowl. Add the egg, then slowly pour in the water or milk and water, stirring and then beating, to give a smooth batter, the consistency of heavy cream. Set aside for about 1 hour.

Oil a griddle or heavy frying pan and heat over a medium heat. Pour about 3 tbsp of batter into the pan, rotating the pan so the batter flows evenly over the surface. Cook until bubbles appear and burst on the surface and the underside is light golden brown. Serve immediately or transfer to a large plate and keep warm while frying the remaining batter.

Arrange the crepes in an overlapping circle around the plate, rather than stacking them as this makes them tough. Serve warm with melted butter, and warm honey flavored with orange-flower water, trickled over.

LEFT *Peach Salad*

Cornstarch Dessert

———— MUHALLABEYA ————

Muhallabeya traveled to North Africa from the Middle East. It has a soothing, silky-light, not-quite-set texture. Instead of the almond and pistachio decoration, almonds can be fried until brown and crisp, then crushed and mixed with a little cinnamon and sugar.

SERVES 4–6

5 tbsp cornstarch

about 3–5 tbsp sugar to
   taste

3 cups full milk

2 tbsp orange-flower water

½ tsp grated lemon zest, if
   liked

⅓ cup mixed blanched
   almonds and pistachios

In a jug, blend the cornstarch and sugar to a paste with a little of the milk. Bring the remaining milk to the boil, stir a little of the boiling milk into the cornstarch mixture, then stir the cornstarch mixture into the simmering milk. Cook, stirring constantly, until thick enough to coat the back of a spoon.

Remove from the heat, stir in the orange-flower water and lemon zest, if used. Pour into a large serving dish, or individual dishes and leave until a skin forms on the surface. Sprinkle over the nuts. Leave until cold, then cover and chill.

Sourdough Starter

In the past, fresh yeast was scarce, or unavailable in North Africa, so a natural sourdough starter was used for making breads. The mixture of flour and water is activated by wild yeasts in the atmosphere and left to ferment before being added to the bread dough. The starter can be kept alive for years – either just a portion is used to make a loaf and the rest replenished with more flour and water, or part of the bread dough is reserved to serve as the next batch of starter.

1 cup all-purpose flour

2 tbsp cornmeal (polenta)

1 tbsp groundnut oil

½–⅔ cup lukewarm
   water

Sift the flour and cornmeal (polenta) together into a bowl. Stir in the oil and ½ cup water to form a smooth dough. Transfer to a work surface and knead in 1–2 tbsp water. Knead for 10–15 minutes until the dough is smooth, shiny, and elastic.

Sprinkle the dough with a little flour and form into a ball that can be held in the hands. Put it in a lightly oiled bowl, cover and leave for 12–24 hours until double in bulk. The starter is now ready to use.

Rice Dessert

ROZ BIL HALIB

Rice dessert is popular throughout North Africa so it's not surprising that the people there really do know how to make a good recipe. Cooked very gently for a long time, the rice is coaxed into absorbing plenty of milk, which makes a very creamy dessert. Almonds are often added to give more flavor; traditionally, the nuts would be pounded into almond milk by hand, but these days can be ground in a blender with hot water, straining the result, then repeating the process. A quicker and easier way is just to add freshly ground almonds to the dessert, with extra milk, which will make it even creamier and more flavorsome, and with a different texture.

SERVES 4
approximately 4½ cups milk
¼ cup dessert (short-grain) rice, rinsed and drained
¼ cup sugar
1–1½ tbsp orange-flower or rose water
chopped pistachio nuts or almonds, crystalized violets or roses

Heat the milk in a heavy, preferably non-stick, saucepan. Sprinkle over the rice and sugar and bring to the boil, stirring. Lower the heat then cook very gently stirring occasionally until the pudding is thick, velvety and falls easily from the spoon – this may take anything up to 2 hours; use a heat diffusing mat, if necessary, to prevent the rice cooking too quickly, and sticking. Stir in orange-flower water or rose water to taste. Pour into a serving dish, or individual dishes. Serve warm or cold with pistachio nuts, almonds, crystalized violets or rose petals scattered over.

LEFT *Wall painting near Tamanrasset, Algeria*

109

Moroccan Bread

KISRA/KHBOZ

Moroccan bread is round, golden and crisp-crusted. Country cooks often use all
barley flour or cornmeal, or a mixture of two or three flours.

MAKES 2 LOAVES, WITH
1 LEFT TO USE AS A STARTER
(OR FERMENTATION ELEMENT)

4 cups strong flour
4 tbsp cornmeal (polenta)
salt

1 quantity Sourdough
*   Starter (see page 108)*
about 1¾ cups warm
*   water*
sesame seeds or aniseed, if
*   liked, for sprinkling*

Sift the flour, cornmeal and salt into a bowl. Add the Sourdough Starter then gradually mix in the water to make a smooth, pliable dough. Beat well then knead for 10–20 minutes until firm and elastic and the dough pulls away cleanly from the sides of the bowl.

Divide the dough into three; reserve one piece to use as a starter. With oiled hands, form the other two pieces into balls, sift a little flour over each then flatten to make 5 inch discs. Place on a floured baking sheet, cover and leave to rise until the dough springs back when pressed.

Preheat the oven to 400°. Prick each loaf three or four times with a fork, sprinkle with sesame seeds or aniseed if liked and bake for about 50 minutes until crisp and golden.

Light Buttery Cookies

GHORIBA SABLE AU BEURRE

These Tunisian pastries show the French influence, both in name and in the use
of butter. They can be flavored with orange-flower or rose water.

MAKES ABOUT 30
3 cups all-purpose flour
pinch of salt
1½ cups powdered sugar,
*   plus extra for sprinkling*

½ cup butter, chopped,
*   melted, and cooled*

Sift the flour and salt into a bowl and make a well in the center. Slowly pour in the melted butter, gradually drawing in the dry ingredients to make a smooth dough. Shape into a ball, cover and chill.

Lightly butter two baking sheets. Knead the dough on a lightly floured surface until soft. Roll walnut-sized pieces into balls and press between your palms to flatten. Place well apart on the baking sheets. Chill for 20–30 minutes.

Preheat the oven to 350°F. Bake the cookies for 10–15 minutes until golden. Leave to cool on a wire rack then dust with powdered sugar.

RIGHT *Moroccan Bread*

Raisin Doughnuts

———— SFENAJ ————

In Morocco the enticing smell of the doughnut-maker beckons people for their breakfast or a street snack. But making sfenaj *is not the prerogative of street doughnut-makers; they can easily be produced at home.*

SERVES 4–6

2 cups sugar
1²⁄₃ cups plus 4 tbsp water
3 tbsp orange-flower water
2 cups strong white flour
2 tbsp lemon juice
pinch of salt
1½ tsp easy blend yeast
⅛ cup raisins
1 egg
oil for deep frying

In a saucepan, gently heat the sugar and 1²⁄₃ cups of water, stirring until the sugar has dissolved. Raise the heat and boil until the syrup has reduced by one third. Remove from the heat and stir in the orange-flower water and lemon juice. Leave to cool.

Sieve the flour with salt into a mixing bowl, then stir in the yeast and raisins. Make a well in the center.

In a jug lightly beat the egg with the remaining water then slowly pour into the well, drawing in the dry ingredients to make a smooth, soft dough, adding more water if necessary. Cover and leave until doubled in volume.

Turn the dough onto a floured surface and knead gently for 5 minutes. Divide the dough into 12 even pieces and roll each piece into a ball. Flatten the balls lightly and make a hole in the center.

In a deep fryer or deep, sturdy saucepan, heat the oil to 350° and fry a few doughnuts at a time for 5–8 minutes until golden. Using a slotted spoon transfer the doughnuts to paper towels to drain. Put them in a bowl, pour over the orange-flower water syrup and leave to soak for about 2 hours.

ABOVE *Dyeing vats in Fez, Medina, Morocco*

112

Almond Pastry Snake

—— M'HANNCHA ——

The Moroccan name for this rich, lightly perfumed pastry, means "the snake,"
accurately describing its coiled shape. M'hanncha will keep for several days if
stored in an airtight container in a cool place, but not the refrigerator. Reheat
gently before serving, if liked.

MAKES 12 PIECES
2 cups ground almonds
1¼ cups powdered sugar
1 egg, separated
few drops of almond
   essence
1½ tbsp rose water

powdered sugar for
   sprinkling
6 sheets filo pastry
4 tbsp melted butter or
   olive oil
powdered sugar and ground
   cinnamon, to decorate

Stir the ground almonds and powdered sugar together in a mixing bowl, then mix to a paste with the egg white, almond essence and rose water. Divide into 3 equal pieces. Sift powdered sugar over the work surface then roll out each piece of almond paste to a 19 inch long sausage, about ½ inch thick.

Brush a sheet of filo pastry with melted butter or oil then cover with a second sheet of pastry and brush that with butter or oil; cover the unused pastry with a damp cloth. Place one almond sausage along the length of the buttered or oiled pastry, about 1 inch from the edge. Roll up the pastry enclosing the almond sausage.

Form into a loose coil starting in the center of a buttered or oiled 8 inch round loose-bottomed flan tin. Repeat with the remaining almond sausages and pastry. Join one to the end of the coil in the tin, and continue the coil outwards, then repeat with the last piece. Beat the egg yolk, in a small bowl, with a pinch of ground cinnamon, then brush over the top. Bake in a preheated oven 350° for about 30 minutes until golden and crisp on top.

Remove the sides of the tin, carfully turn the coil over, replace on the bottom of the tin and return to the oven for a further 10 minutes, until the bottom is brown. Invert on to a cooling rack and leave to cool slightly. Sift over powdered sugar then add lines of ground cinnamon to form a lattice pattern. Serve warm, cut into wedges.

Crisp Almond and Sesame Pastries

————— SAMSA —————

Like all Arab pastries, these from Tunisia are very sweet and only one or two can be eaten at a time. Fortunately, they do keep well when stored in an airtight container.

MAKES ABOUT 24

⅔ cup sugar
1¼ cup water
1 tbsp lemon juice
orange-flower water
1½ cups blanched almonds, lightly toasted and ground
1½ tsp finely grated orange zest
1½ tsp ground cinnamon, if liked
about 4 oz filo pastry
olive oil, for brushing
lightly toasted sesame seeds for sprinkling

Put the water and ½ cup of the sugar in a saucepan and heat gently, stirring until dissolved. Add the lemon juice and boil until syrupy. Remove from the heat and add the orange-flower water. Leave to cool.

Preheat the oven to 350°. In a mixing bowl, stir together the ground almonds, orange zest, cinnamon if using, and remaining sugar, then knead together the ingredients.

Brush one sheet of filo with olive oil; keep the other sheets covered with a damp cloth. Cut the oiled sheet into 3 lengthways strips. Place a small spoonful of filling at the bottom of each strip.

Fold the sides over the filling then roll the pastry up along the length. Brush inside the end of the pastry with oil and seal it to the roll. Brush with oil and put on a baking sheet. Repeat with the remaining pastry and filling. Bake the pastries for 15–20 minutes until crisp and golden.

Lower the pastries a few at a time into the hot syrup, leave for about 3 minutes so the syrup penetrates the pastries, then remove to a plate and sprinkle generously with sesame seeds. Leave until cold before serving.

ABOVE *Roman Amphitheatre, El Djem, Tunisia*

114

Pitta Bread

———— PITA ————

Although packets of ready-baked pitta bread are now available in North Africa, some people still make their own dough and take it, ready-shaped to a baker, or buy freshly baked bread from small shops, what are little more than kiosks in the streets.

The dough can be flavored with ground cumin or herbs, or brushed after shaping with good olive oil and sprinkled with sesame seeds, or plenty of "za'atar" mixed with salt.

To obtain the characteristic hollow, puffed shape, a very hot oven is needed (traditionally this would be wood-fired), so be sure to turn the oven on well in advance to give it plenty of time to heat up, but even then, some ovens may not reach the necessary temperature. I also recommend preheating the baking trays for 2 minutes. Alternatively, the breads can be cooked under a very hot broiler.

MAKES ABOUT 12

½ oz fresh yeast or 1½ tsp easy-blend yeast
pinch of sugar, (if liked)
approximately 1 cup warm water
4 cups unbleached strong white flour
salt
1 tbsp olive oil, plus extra for brushing

Put the fresh yeast in a bowl, and if using with the sugar, blend in a little of the water then leave until frothy. Sieve the flour and a pinch of salt into a bowl. Stir in the easy-blend yeast, if using. Form a well in the center. Pour the yeast liquid, if using, remaining water and the oil into the well and gradually draw the dry ingredients into the liquids, first using a wooden spoon then your hand. Mix to form firm, soft dough.

Turn the dough onto a lightly floured surface and knead for about 15 minutes until smooth and elastic. Generously oil a bowl, put the dough into it then turn the dough over to coat with oil. Cover and leave at room temperature until doubled in volume.

Turn the dough onto the work surface and knead briefly. Divide into 12 equal pieces. Flatten each piece with the palm of your hand to about ¼ inch thick and 4 inches in diameter. Brush with oil and place well apart on baking sheets. Cover with a lightly floured cloth and leave to rise for about 20 minutes. Preheat the oven to its highest setting.

Dampen the top of each piece of dough with cold water to prevent it browning. If cooking in the oven, using a spatula, transfer some of the shapes to an oiled, preheated baking tray and bake for about 3 minutes, then lower the thermostat to 450° and bake for a further 2–3 minutes, until puffed and lightly speckled with brown.

If using the broiler place the pieces of bread in turn under a very hot preheated broiler, leaving them space to rise, and cook until puffed up and speckled with brown. Turn over immediately and leave for about 1 minute more.

Seal bread that is not to be eaten straight away in a plastic bag while still warm. For longer storage, freeze it, then reheat from frozen under the broiler or in the oven. Bread that becomes dry can be refreshed by sprinkling with water then warming under a preheated broiler or in the oven. To keep several loaves hot, wrap them in foil and put in the oven.

8

Spice Mixes, Sauces, and Drinks

As alcohol is forbidden under Islam, other drinks replace wine. With such luscious fruits available, fruit juices and fruit-based drinks are popular. In Morocco sweet Mint Tea is *the* drink. Tea-making and drinking are taken very seriously and the whole process is surrounded by ritual and ceremony. Tea is drunk throughout the day, including at the end of a meal, anywhere, by any age group, for many contradictory reasons – as a restorative or sedative, as a medicine or a placebo.

Moroccan Spice Mix

—— RAS EL HANOUT ——

This recipe for fragrant spice mix (see page 11) has been simplified, which means it does, of course, lack some of the glory of a more complex blend.

MAKES ABOUT
2½ TABLESPOONS
6 allspice berries
4 cloves
1½ tsp black peppercorns

1¼ tsp coriander seeds
1 tsp cumin seeds
¼ tsp cayenne pepper
1½ tsp ground cinnamon
1 tsp ground ginger

Put all the whole spices in a grinder or pestle and mortar and work to a powder. Mix in the ground spices, then spoon into a glass bottle. Keep in a cool, dark place.

Za'atar

Za'atar can be mixed to a paste with olive oil and spread on bread before baking, used as a dip, and sprinkled on vegetables and meat balls. The blend can be stored for 3–4 months.

2 oz sesame seeds
1 oz powdered dried thyme

1 oz ground sumac

Heat the sesame seeds in a dry heavy frying pan, stirring frequently, until very lightly toasted. Allow to cool then mix with the thyme and sumac. Store in an airtight jar in a cool, dry, dark place.

Tunisian Five Spices

—— QALAT DAGGA ——

This blend is used in vegetable and lamb dishes. The spice called grains of paradise (Melegueta pepper) is a member of the cardamom family. The spice mix will keep for 3–4 months.

2 tsp cloves
2 tsp black peppercorns
1 tsp grains of paradise

1 tsp ground cinnamon
1 tsp freshly grated nutmeg

Grind the cloves, peppercorns and grains of paradise together in a grinder or pestle and mortar then mix with the other spices. Keep in an airtight jar in a cool, dry, dark place.

Tabil

Tabil *means coriander, but generally refers to this Tunisian spice blend, which includes coriander.*

2 tbsp coriander seeds
1 tbsp caraway seeds
4 garlic cloves

2 tsp crushed dried red chili

Preheat the oven to its lowest setting. Pound all the ingredients together in a pestle and mortar, then spread over a baking tray and put in the oven for about 30 minutes until dry. Grind the dry ingredients to a fine powder. Keep in an airtight container for up to 4 months.

Harissa

Or "arhissa" as it is sometimes called, is a fiery paste based on chilies. It is primarily associated with Tunisia but it is also used in Algeria and Morocco. As well as being served as a condiment at the table, in a small dish with a small spoon, Harissa is used in cooking to add life to meat, poultry or vegetable casseroles, saffron-flavored fish soups and stews, "stewed" red peppers and tomatoes. It is often used as a base for poached eggs, or added to dips, sauces and salad dressings.

*2 oz dried red chilies,
    soaked in hot water for
    1 hour
2 garlic cloves, chopped
2 tsp coriander seeds*

*2 tsp cumin seeds
2 tsp caraway seeds
pinch of salt
6 tbsp olive oil*

Drain the chilies and put in a mortar, spice grinder or small blender with the garlic, spices, and salt. Mix to a paste then stir in 3 tbsp of olive oil. Transfer to a small jar and pour a little oil over the surface. Cover and keep in a cool, dark place, or the refrigerator for 4–6 weeks.

Moroccan Butter

——— SMEN ———

This is a simplified way of making smen *(see page 11).*

*2 cups sweet butter, diced
1 tbsp coarse salt*

¼ tsp herbes de
    Provence

Gently heat the butter in a saucepan until melted, then bring to the boil. Lower the heat and simmer for 3–4 minutes until the butter is clear and there is a separate layer on the bottom of the pan.

Line a sieve with muslin that has been wrung out in hot water, and sprinkle with the salt and herb. Gradually spoon the clear butter into the sieve and allow it to strain through. Then strain it again into a clean, dry jar. Cover and keep in the refrigerator for up to 6 weeks.

RIGHT *Harissa*

Almond Milk

SHARBAT BIL LOOZ

For the cleanest flavor, be sure to use fresh almonds.

SERVES 3–4

1 cup cold milk

1½ cups whole blanched
  almonds

1 cup chilled water

fine granulated sugar, to
  taste

rose water or orange-flower
  water, to taste

Mix the milk and almonds together in a blender until smooth. Strain through a sieve, pressing down hard on the sieve to extract as much liquid as possible.

Add the water to the almond milk then stir in sugar until it dissolves, and add rose water or orange-flower to taste. Chill before serving.

Apple Milkshake

SARBAT

A rich, cool drink made from milk and fruit or nut milk, sarbat *is an ideal "pick-me-up" for serving in the late afternoon on hot days when dinner will be late and something is needed to sustain guests through the early evening.*

SERVES 2–4

2 dessert apples, peeled,
  cored, and chopped

2 cups cold milk

2 tbsp caster sugar

about 1½ tsp rose water or
  orange-flower water

shaved ice, to serve, if liked

Put the apples, milk, and sugar into a blender and mix until smooth. Add rose water or orange-flower water to taste. Serve over shaved ice, if liked, in chilled glasses.

Mint Tea

ETZAI

This light, sweet tea, particularly popular in Morocco, is made with green China tea and fresh spearmint. It is served as part of the traditional ritual of hospitality and the silver tea pot, sugar bowl and tray, the samovar and the ornately painted glasses and tea table can be quite magnificent.

1½ tbsp green tea
boiling water
3 tbsp sugar, or to taste

handful or fresh spearmint leaves

Put the tea in a 2 pint tea pot. Pour in a cupful of boiling water then immediately pour it out again; this is to wash the leaves. Add the sugar to taste, and the mint leaves. Pour in boiling water from a height of 12 inches (this oxygenates the made tea) and stir well. Serve the tea very hot, again pouring it from a height of about 12 inches.

LEFT *Apple Milkshake*

Lemons Preserved in Oil

This is an alternative way of preserving lemons, rather than packing them with salt (see opposite). The lemons are used to great effect with firm white fish (see Bream with Preserved Lemons, page 50). This recipe also works very well with limes.

4 large lemons
salt
few sprigs of cilantro
2 plump garlic cloves,
   lightly crushed

1–2 dried red chilies
olive oil, to cover

Slice the lemons fairly thickly, discarding the pips. Sprinkle with plenty of salt and leave in a colander for 24 hours. Rinse and dry the lemons then pack into a clean, dry jar, inserting the cilantro, garlic, and chilies down the side of the jar as you go. Pour in olive oil to well cover the lemons. Swivel the jar to dispel any air bubbles. Cover the jar and leave for at least 1 month, swivelling the jar occasionally.

Preserved Lemons

Lemons lose their sharpness when preserved in salt and their unique flavor and silken texture is a characteristic of North African, and especially Moroccan, cooking. They also make a novel addition to non-Moroccan dishes. Preserved Lemons are easy to prepare; I have given two versions – one plain and the other with the less commonly used Safi spice mixture. Thin-skinned lemons will yield more juice. Once the jar has been opened the lemons will keep for up to a year, out of the refrigerator, but a layer of olive oil floated on the surface will help to preserve their freshness.

coarse salt	*plump, juicy lemons, preferably thin-skinned*

Put 2 tsp coarse salt in a scalded Kilner or Parfait jar. Holding a lemon over a plate to catch the juice, and using a sharp, stainless-steel knife, cut lengthways as if about to halve the fruit, but do not cut quite through – leave the pieces joined. Ease out any pips. Pack 1 tbsp salt into the cuts, then close them and put in the jar. Repeat with more lemons, packing them tightly and pressing each layer down hard before adding the next layer, until the jar is full.

Squeeze the juice of another lemon over the fruit. Sprinkle with more coarse salt and top up with boiling water to cover the fruit. Close the jar tightly and keep in a warmish place for 3–4 weeks. Do not worry if, on longer storage, a lacy white film appears on top of the jar or on the lemons, this is quite harmless, and rinses off easily.

Note: If liked, a mixture of 1 stick of cinnamon, 3 cloves, 6 crushed coriander seeds, 3 black peppercorns, and 1 bay leaf can be layered with the lemons.

Chermoula 1

This is a recipe for a simple, basic all-purpose chermoula *that you can use as a starting point to create your own versions for specific purposes. For example, you can increase the amount of parsley, cilantro, or chili, add finely chopped or grated onion, or adjust the ratio of the other spices.*

ENOUGH TO MARINATE A FISH
FOR 4 PEOPLE, OR MAKE A
SAUCE FOR 4

3 garlic cloves
salt
¼ dried red chili, chopped
1½ tbsp paprika
1½ tbsp ground cumin

3 tbsp chopped fresh
   cilantro
3 tbsp chopped fresh
   parsley
1 tbsp lemon juice
3½ tbsp white-wine
   vinegar
1½ tbsp fruity olive oil

Put the garlic, salt, and chili into a grinder and mix to a paste. Mix in the ground spices and herbs then add the lemon juice, vinegar and oil until smooth. Heat gently in a saucepan until hot and fragrant, but do not allow to boil. Leave to cool before using.

Chermoula 2

This is a more robust version of the chermoula *recipe above.*

ENOUGH TO MARINATE FISH,
POULTRY OR MEAT FOR
4 PEOPLE

1 red onion, finely chopped
2 plump garlic cloves,
   finely chopped
pinch saffron threads,
   lightly toasted and
   crushed

½ tsp ground cumin
¼ tsp paprika
pinch of cayenne
1 small bunch of mixed
   parsley and cilantro,
   chopped
juice of ½ lemon
6 tbsp olive oil
salt

Mix all the ingredients together, as in the above recipe.

Index

Picture Credits for location photography

Nick Bailey: pages 6, 14, 18, 19, 26, 32, 34, 54, 85, 90, 101, 104, 109, 112, 114
Life File: pages 7, 9, 10, 12, 45, 86